PUB WALKS
IN WEST SU

Forty Circular Walks

Around West Sussex Inns

Mike Power

Other books in the series
Pub Walks in Dorset
Forty More Pub Walks in Dorset
Pub Walks in Hampshire and the I.O.W.
Pub Walks in Devon
Pub Walks in Cornwall
Pub Walks in East Sussex
Pub Walks in Kent
Mike Power's Pub Walks in The New Forest

1st Edition - published December 1991
Reprinted - March 1993
2nd Edition - published March 1996

© Power Publications

ISBN 0-9514502-6-3

Publisher's note
Whilst every care has been taken to ensure that all the information given in the book is correct at the time of going to print neither the publishers nor the printers can accept any responsibility for any inaccuracies. We always welcome any comments you wish to make regarding our publications especially when changes have taken place as our books our periodically up-dated.

Power Publications
1, Clayford Ave
Ferndown
Dorset. BH22 9PQ

Maps: Mike Power
Photographs: Mike Power
Cover photograph: John Botel
Printed by Pardy & Son (Printers) Ltd Ringwood, Hants.
Front cover: The Shepherd & Dog Fulking

Introduction

Before writing this book I had seen very little of West Sussex. From what I had read, and been told by others, I knew the county possessed some of the most delightful countryside and villages in Britain, a fact which I now know to be true. During my research I travelled the length and breadth of the county, discovered many delightful places, visited numerous attractive pubs and eventually devised interesting walks around forty of the best. The pubs are all in rural locations, some are on the coast the rest tucked peacefully away well off the beaten track. They have been chosen either for their location or their charm, no charge is made for inclusion in the book. The walks are planned to start from the pub in which case one assumes you would wish to partake of their hospitality, on the rare occasion you might not we respectfully ask you to refrain from using their car park; where possible we have indicated suitable alternatives but of course there is no reason why you should not start from any point along the route. The walks, all circular, vary in length from $2\frac{1}{2}$ miles to 8 miles, and are explained in detail each with an accompanying sketch map.

They appeal very much to families, perhaps walking for the first time, who can choose how far they want to walk, know in advance the conditions they are likely to encounter with the added incentive of finishing at a nice pub. It has been proved that walking is extremely good for you; it is also safe providing a few simple rules are observed. Try to wear suitable clothing. Lightweight but waterproof long trousers or leggings are best, although tempting on a warm summer day to walk in shorts, many of the paths become overgrown with nettles and other nasties. A waterproof jacket or cagoule is an essential item as are strong waterproof boots but any stout comfortable footwear will do provided it is well treaded.

Take care when walking along country roads without pavements; always walk facing the oncoming traffic except on a dangerous right-hand bend. The majority of paths in West Sussex are well maintained, well marked and walked on a regular basis but it is still a good idea to carry the relevant Ordnance Survey map with you. The map reference at the beginning of each walk refers to the 1:50 000 - $1\frac{1}{4}$ inch to 1 mile in the Landranger series. The three you will need to cover the walks in this book are nos.187, 197, and 198. For more detailed maps there is also the Pathfinder series they cover an area of 1:25 000 - $2\frac{1}{2}$ inches to the mile but you will require many more of them.

I always carry a stick: it is ideal for clearing brambles and overgrown paths, it can be used to test the stability of the ground ahead and most important it can be waved in the air to deter animals.

The 'Rights of Way Act', which came into force on August 13 1990, has much improved the rights of ramblers; it was a massive step forward in path protection. The act requires occupiers who disturb the land to make good the surface within 24 hours of the disturbance or two weeks if the disturbance is the first one for a particular crop. Where no width is recorded the minimum width of a path must be one metre and two metres for a bridleway and the exact line of the path must be apparent on the ground. Furthermore the occupier must prevent crops growing on, or encroaching onto the path. You should report any problems you find to the relevant authority. Wherever you go in the country always remember the code. Guard against fires, fasten all gates, keep dogs under control and always on a lead where livestock are present. Keep to the paths across farm land, take your litter home and never pick wild flowers or dig up the plants. I very much enjoyed all the walks in this book, I hope you will too.

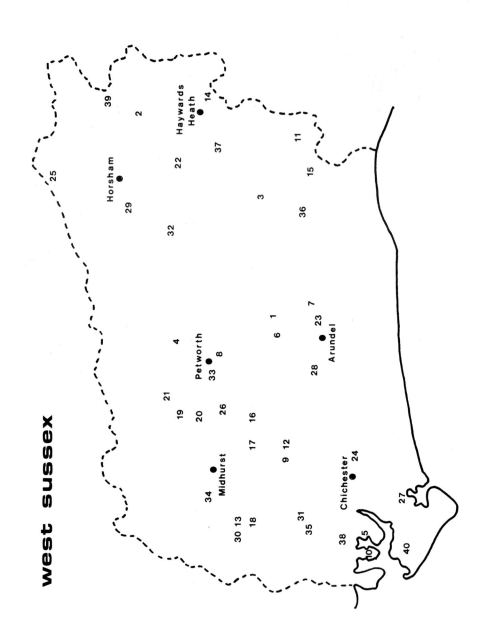

The Black Horse, Amberley

Amberley Village is often called the 'Pearl of Sussex'. It is in a delightful position with The Downs to the south and Amberley Wild Brooks to the north. There are many pretty cottages, some are very old timber framed buildings with the inside walls of wattle and daub. The Black Horse was once several cottages which were knocked through to form the present three rooms. The 'village bar', reached up a flight of steps, is simply furnished and heated in winter by a warm coal fire. There are rugs on the flag stone floor, lots of old photographs around the walls and, hanging from the beamed ceiling, an interesting collection of old sheep bells once owned by Frank Oliver the last shepherd from the village. On the right is a comfortable seating area. Another smaller bar has high back wooden settles and also a warm coal fire. A bistro at the back of the inn can seat up to sixty and more people can be accommodated on wooden chairs and tables in the beer garden where there is a large enclosed pond and aviary.

The inn is part of Allied Brewery at present serving two well conditioned real ales, Friary Mieux Best Bitter and Flowers Original plus some seasonal additions.

Good home cooked bar food is available seven days a week. Apart from snacks such as mushrooms in garlic and king size ploughman's with a choice of at least eight different cheeses other meals include salads, smoked salmon cornets stuffed with prawns, steak & kidney pie, king prawns in garlic and chicken breast in white wine with a cream of tarragon sauce together with a couple of vegetarian dishes. A more comprehensive restaurant menu has a choice of six starters followed by locally caught fresh grilled plaice, and for the summer crab and lobster salads. Several chicken dishes include 'Mexican', very hot with peppers onions and garlic and succulent steaks offered with a choice of sauces like Port and Stilton or peppered with brandy and cream.

Children are allowed away from the bar and dogs too are welcome.

Weekday opening times are from 11 a.m. (10.30 a.m. Saturday) till 3 p.m. and 6 p.m. till 11 p.m. Old Sunday hours.

Telephone: (01798) 831552 or 831700.

The village is signed off the B2139 reached from either the A29 or the A283.

Approx. distance of walk: 5 miles. OS Map No. 197 TQ 032/133.

Park where you can in the village.

A very enjoyable level walk from this delightful village at first through woods to the tiny hamlet of Greatham and then back beside the River Arun and across Amberley Wild Brooks. Try to avoid this walk in the winter the brooks are often flooded and difficult to negotiate.

1. Turn right from the pub and walk up the lane past the many delightful houses with their lovely gardens and admire the wild flowers both in the gardens and growing from crevises in the walls. Continue through the village, and just beyond the last house on the left, go over the stile in the hedge on the left. Bear left across the field to the stile in the far hedge, cross the plank bridge and head for the stile in the corner. The path bears left and then heads through a small wood to a stile. It is very attractive but can become overgrown in summer.

2. Keeping to the right of the building, bear left across the grass to the ridge. Cross the stile and make your way over the meadow to the bridge in the distance. Go over into the wood and take the signed path on the left. Eventually you reach a finger post which directs you to the right. Keep to the grass path turning left into the lane.

3. Turn left when you reach the T junction at Greatham. A short de-tour ahead will take you to Greatham Church built during

the reign of King John in the 12th century. Although none of the lanes in the area are particularly busy this one does carry more traffic than most so a little care is necessary. There is a stile on the left just before reaching the bridge. Go up to the river bank then follow the path beside the Arun, over a small stile and into a field following the hedge line round to meet a gravel track. Cross the cattle grid and turn right.

4. Bear left past the farm buildings, through the farmyard and turn right onto the track, it is signed. Go through the farm gate and, keeping close to the right-hand hedge, walk down to the bottom of the field and over the plank bridges. The exact path is not well defined but keep to a straight line following the ridge where possible until you reach the stile.

5. Follow the track ahead up to the lane and turn left back to the pub. Amberley is such a pretty village it is well worth a walk round before leaving just to see the houses.

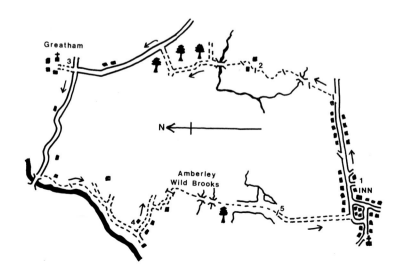

The Oak Inn, Ardingly

The Oak is a very old pub; the main building itself dates back to the fourteenth century. The lovely 'Oak Bar' has a heavily beamed ceiling and a large inglenook fireplace with built-in seats. All round the walls and on the beams are masses of brightly shining copper items and horse brasses. Drinks are served from a large hatch in one wall. On the other side of the hallway are two more attractive beamed dining areas and more seats in a restaurant beside the food servery. The attractive front garden has several wooden tables and benches with more picnic benches on the lawn at the side. The pub and gardens are all beautifully kept, so much so that in 1990 it was voted runner up in the country section of the West Sussex 'Pub of the Year' competition run by the Evening Argos.

The inn is a free house offering one a choice of various guest ales.

The Oak Inn is a popular place to eat; busy all week with diners. Food is available seven days a week from 12 noon till 2.30 p.m. and again from 7 p.m. till 9.30 p.m. Ordered from the servery and selected from the set menu or the specials board, snacks include soup of the day, sandwiches, ploughman's and a choice of platters, 'Oak' platter has a Stilton wedge, honey roast ham and prawns in a Marie-Rose sauce and 'Vikings' platter is home cooked ham and turkey breast plus a hot jumbo sausage. The set menu offers a choice of starters plus steaks, various fish dishes and 'tramps dinner' which is simply sausage, egg, baked beans and chips. There is a childrens' menu for the under 10's. Daily specials might include various pies of country chicken, steak and kidney and chicken and asparagus also cod and prawn provencale, haddock hot pot and turkey and mushrooms in red wine.

Weekday opening times are from 11 a.m. till 11 p.m. Sunday 12 noon till 10.30 p.m.

Children are only allowed in the dining area and dogs only in the Oak Bar. Telephone: (01444) 892244.

Village reached from the B2028, north from Crawley Down or south from Haywards Heath. The pub is located in Street Lane.

Approx. distance of walk: 5 miles. OS Map No. 187 TQ 347/295.

Parking is a bit restricted at the pub but there is space in the road opposite or in various places around the village.

A very enjoyable scenic walk, hilly in places, through woodland and around the banks of Ardingly Reservoir. The walk passes close to Wakehurst Place, the grounds of which are open daily from 10 a.m.

1. Leave the pub, cross the road and turn left. In a quarter of a mile go through the gate on the right of the church and turn left keeping to the main concrete road through the show ground. Pass through a gate and further on leave the show ground by the iron gate bearing left onto the track. Go through the gate and keep straight ahead joining with another track then make your way down to the stile beside the gate at the bottom.

2. Keep to the right-hand hedge boundary, in a hundred yards go through the farm gate and continue ahead downhill to the stile, through the trees into the field beyond and follow the field boundary to the stile in the fence. The path bears left through woodland before reaching the bridge across the Ardingly Reservoir. On the far side turn right, climb the stile into woodland and follow the path uphill eventually turning right into the lane.

3. After about half a mile and upon reaching the brow of the hill take the track on the left and in fifty yards go over the stile beside the gate, ignore the track to the right. Walk down the field to the stile in the bottom left-hand corner, go over into the field ahead and maintain direction, over another stile and turn right. After crossing the stile in the bottom right-hand corner turn left onto the farm track.

4. Once past the lake look for a stile in the hedge on the left, go into the field and straight ahead to the plank bridge, then cross the stile. Keeping close to the hedge, go over another stile, through the trees, out into the road and turn left. Cross the bridge and walk up the hill until you reach a gate on the right. Bear half left and follow the bridleway keeping to the main path into the field and down to the shore of the reservoir.

5. At the lane go over the stile, turn right to cross the causeway, over another stile and back down to the banks of the reservoir. In a quarter of a mile there is a stile on the left, the path is marked on a stone at the side. Go over, up to a second stile and continue up the field to the stile in the top left-hand corner. Follow the track taking time as you go to look back and enjoy the view. Continue uphill crossing the stile before eventually reaching the church then turn right at the junction back to the pub.

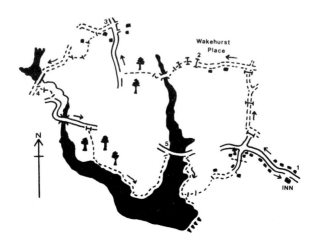

The Fountain Inn, Ashurst

Ashurst is very much agricultural in character with a small population, among the more famous residents is Lady Olivier wife of the late Lord Olivier. The lovely Fountain Inn, which dates in part back to the sixteenth century, was voted best country pub in West Sussex by The Evening Argos as recently as 1990. Another claim to fame happened several years ago when Paul McCartney and Wings used the pub to record their hit Christmas song 'Having a Jolly Good Christmas'. The aptly named, low beamed 'Inglenook Bar' has one of the largest inglenook fireplaces in any pub in the county. There are simple furnishings on the original scrubbed flag stone floor and a unique hatched bar allows service from either of three hatchways. A passageway leads through to the larger carpeted lounge. There is a function room/skittle alley, two large beer gardens, one with a childrens' play area, barbecue and picnic benches amongst the apple trees, the other having benches on a gravel terrace beside a duck pond.

The inn is a free house and the landlord, Maurice Caine, is particularly interested in stocking a good range of real ales. Rotated regularly are John Smith's, Courage Best and Directors Bitter, Fullers London Pride, Young's Special and Adnams Extra and Broadside.

Good food, home cooked by the landlord's wife, is available daily from 12.00 noon. Traditional pub snacks include soup and ploughman's plus simple dishes like steak and kidney pudding, suet and bacon pudding, cauliflower cheese, cottage pie, rogan josh, quiches, flans and pizza. The evening menu, available from 7 p.m. except Sunday in the candle-lit dining room, is upgraded slightly to include various steaks, chicken Kiev and turkey cordon bleu. The sweet menu lists puddings like apricot crumble.

Children are allowed in the lounge if eating with their parents. Dogs are permitted in the inglenook bar and garden.

Weekday opening times are from 11 a.m. till 2.30 p.m. and 6 p.m. till 11 p.m. Sunday 12 noon till 2.30 p.m. and 7 p.m. till 10.30 p.m.

Telephone: (01403) 710219

Ashurst is on the B2135 just south of Partridge Green.

Approx. distance of walk 5 miles. OS Map No.198 TQ 179/162.

The inn has its own car park but there is additional parking at the village hall.

A fairly level and easy walk on peaceful lanes, farm tracks and footpaths with pleasant country views.

1. From the pub cross the road and go over the stile to the left of the telephone kiosk. Keeping close to the hedge on the right, walk down to the stile and continue ahead, out into the lane turning right. Walk up the rise past the 12th century parish church of St James keeping straight ahead at the junction. When you reach Ford Farm the path has been diverted to the left. Follow the path between the tractor shed and the house passing down between the barns and onto the track. In twenty yards turn right in the direction of the finger post walking beside the fence then bear left at the top of the hill following the fence round to the right. In fifty yards turn left keeping to the track down towards the river. Ignore the gate ahead but turn right through the hedge, under the electricity wires then left through the hedge.

2. Cross the iron bridge over the River Adur, go through the gate and along the hedgerow towards the farm. Further on pass through the gate keeping straight ahead on the farm track then turn left at the junction through an open gateway. Keep walking until a gate allows access to the lane. Follow the road round the bend, ignoring the fist signed path and the stile into private woods, but continue uphill until you reach a footpath on the left. Go through the open gateway and across the field, through the gap in the hedge opposite then up the field making your way towards the barn. Leave by the gate and turn left walking behind the building towards the electricity pole with the grey transformer. Go over the stile, down the bank, over another stile onto the track and turn right. Bear left at the white house, go out into the lane and turn left.

3. Turn right when you reach the track to Daylands Farm. Keep straight ahead for almost a mile then go through the gate on the bend and, keeping close to the hedge, walk down the field to the far corner. Cross the stream, pass through the gate into the field following the boundary, then go right, over the fence into the adjoining field and turn left. On the far side go through the gate and turn right through a second gate. At the end of the fence climb the stile, cross the farm road and pass through the gate into the field opposite. Keeping to the hedge boundary walk up to the gate, go through and immediately turn left through a gate onto the farm track. In fifty yards turn left again onto a similar track.

4. When you reach a path junction turn right and join the bridleway then go left through the gate onto the footpath, it is signed. Keeping to the left-hand boundary walk up the field, through the gate at the top and turn right following the hedge to the stile in the corner of the field. Continue over the plank bridge into the field and straight ahead up through a couple of gates then turn right through a third into the field beyond. Walk diagonally across to a gate on the far side, go through, then left through another gate. Bear left across the field to the stile at the far corner, out into the lane and walk straight ahead eventually turning right at the junction. As you pass the school a gap in the hedge on the right allows access to the recreation fields. Walk parallel with the road, out though the iron gate then turn right, down the lane to the road and left back to the pub.

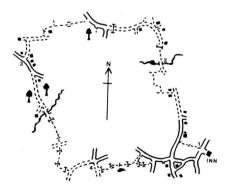

The Stag, Balls Cross

This attractive old stone built village local dates back to the sixteenth century and was once an old coaching inn, the original stables now used as a garage. There are two small bars and an end room. The simply furnished, unspoilt main bar is low ceilinged with the original bare flag stone floor and large inglenook fireplace at one end. The other simply furnished carpeted bar has a warm log fire in winter. At the sunny front of the pub are a few picnic benches with more seating and a childrens' play area on the back lawn.

The inn is owned by King and Barnes, the local Horsham Brewery. They brew a range of five traditional ales two of which are always available. For the summer there is either Sussex, Broadwood, Festive or Mild with Old Ale in the winter. The Stag was the first pub to win the Peter King Memorial Shield - awarded by CAMRA.

A good choice of food, served daily except Sunday evening, includes the usual bar snacks such as sandwiches, ploughman's, summer salads and jackets potatoes. Very popular are their own homemade dishes especially the steak and kidney pie made with stout. Other dishes include trout, chilli, lasagne, moussaka, ham and eggs, curry and a choice of steaks. Children have their own menu and there are usually one or two vegetarian dishes such as vegetable curry, lasagne or macaroni cheese

Children are allowed in the garden or in the end room only. There is no objection to dogs on a lead.

Normal opening times are from 11 a.m. till 2.30 p.m. and 6 p.m. till 11 p.m. Sunday 12 noon till 3 p.m. and 7 p.m. till 10.30 p.m. The only exception if a major event should take place in the area.

Telephone: (01403) 820241.

Leave Petworth north on the A283 and take the right-hand turn signposted, Balls Cross and Kirdford.

Approx. distance of walk: 4 miles. OS Map No. 197 SU 987/263.

Park at the front of the inn, on the grass verge at the side or in the lane.

A mostly level walk, muddy in places, but easy going across farm land and through delightful bluebell woods. Apart from the beginning and end the walk is entirely on bridleways so there are no stiles.

1. Leave the pub and turn right, walk up the hill turning left onto the signed bridleway at Langhurst Farm. The track passes between farm buildings after which it bears right through a farm gateway, and a short distance ahead, passes through a similar gate. Just before reaching a gateway into the field ahead the track bears right down past woods eventually leading into a field at the bottom. On the right is a small gate into a field, the bridleway is signed. Go through and, keeping close to the hedge on the left, make your way to the far corner where you will see a small path on the left leading up to a forest gate.

2. Follow the track through the bluebell wood, up to the junction of the signed bridleway and turn right. Keep to the main track until it emerges onto a gravel track under power lines then turn left and bear right back into woodland. Keep to the main track, ignoring the side turnings, which eventually takes you past Blackbrook Farm onto a metalled drive and out to meet the lane.

3. Cross over and follow the track ahead back into woods keeping straight ahead at the cross track. A lot of the trees are oak and there are often men to be seen cutting and preparing fencing wood. When you reach the junction of three tracks take the one on the left. After a couple of bends it joins with a cross track. Turn left over the stream following it until it joins with a metalled drive at Crowfold Farm then keep straight ahead, up to the main road and turn left. Cross over walking the short distance back to the pub.

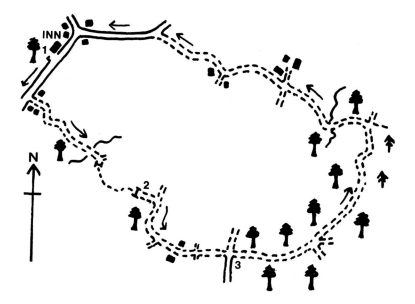

The sketch maps in this book are not necessarily to scale but have been drawn to show the maximum amount of detail.

Anchor Bleu, Bosham

Bosham is a delightful, picturesque old village in an idyllic position on the sea coast. The vast colourful expanse of weed in the creek and the rocking boats on the cool sparkling water have tempted many to put paint to canvas. The Romans landed here during the occupation and built a settlement. It is also thought by many historians that King Canute had a residence in the village. Certainly the story of his daughter being buried in the church proved to be true. The position of this lovely old waterside tavern is quite unique having one side facing inland to the quaint village street whilst the other forms part of the quay itself enabling it to be reached by boat at high tide. It is a listed building and, although mentioned in a schedule of local taverns in 1740, probably dates back to much earlier times. The main bar has a lovely old flagstone floor and a separate partitioned seating area whilst the back room has close-boarded planks. The low beamed ceiling is timber propped in places and there is a fireplace in the side wall. There are padded settles around the walls above which are nautical prints and photographs. Outside there is a front terrace and another overlooking the water.

The inn is owned by Scottish and Newcastle presently offering five real ales Websters Yorkshire Bitter, Ruddles County and Best Bitter, Theakstons and Directors Bitter and a selection of wines from around the world.

Typical pub grub is served between 12 noon and 2 p.m. and includes four daily specials, ploughman's, a selection of meats and four different cheeses etc. with a separate evening menu available between 7 p.m. and 9 p.m.

Weekday opening times are from 11 a.m. till 11 p.m. Sunday 12 noon till 10.30 p.m.

There is no objection to children or dogs.

Telephone: (01243) 573956.

Village signed south from the A27 west of Chichester.

Approx. distance of walk: 3 miles. OS Map No. 197 SU 805/038.

Park only on the shore road if you are certain the tide is on the ebb. Photographs on the wall inside the pub are a daunting reminder of those motorists that got it wrong. If you are uncertain it is probably best to find somewhere else in the village.

Bosham, pronounced 'bozzam', is an interesting spot situated on the edge of an estuary. The waters rise at flood-tide to the sills of the cottage doors and have, in extremely bad conditions, entered many of the cottage including the pub; photographic evidence of which can be seen on the wall. In order to follow the walk it is necessary to first check the tide times. You can telephone the Anchor Bleu. Each day the high water time is chalked on a blackboard in the bar. The walk follows the shore line for only a short part of the way and if you do get caught by the tide there are alternative routes. The rest of the walk is flat, easy going, across farm land and along peaceful country lanes.

1. From the pub walk down to the shore road and turn left walking round until you reach the road at the head of the creek. Turn left and after a few paces go down the signed footpath on the right between the houses. As you emerge beside the cottage cross over the lane, go up the steps in the bank opposite and straight ahead following the raised footpath across the field and into a second. Keeping close to the hedge on the left, walk round until you reach a wooden crossing point in the corner allowing access to a narrow path between the hedge and the wire fence on the right then turn left into the lane.

2. After passing the farm buildings, and at the point where the lane bears to the right, keep straight ahead through the farm gate onto the drive turning left when you join the gravel track. After a short distance cross another gravel track and take the signed footpath to the left of the farm gate running close to the line of trees on the right. Eventually upon reaching the road bear left and keep straight ahead ignoring the left turn to Bosham Hoe.

3. After passing the Millstream Hotel, a lovely place to stop for afternoon tea, take the turning right into Moreton Road, walk down to the bottom and join the signed footpath on the left, past the buildings to the shore and turn left. Walk round keeping close to the sea wall and, after passing a large house but before reaching the sailing club, go up the slipway, out onto the drive and turn right. Leave by the entrance gates walking past the church back to the pub. Holy Trinity is well worth a visit being one of the oldest churches in Sussex. The tower, nave and part of the chancel are Saxon and probably belong to the early part of the 11th century, quite possibly erected under the authority of King Canute.

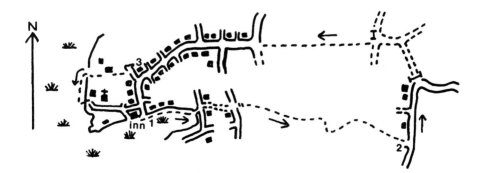

Black Dog & Duck, Bury

Delightfully situated in a peaceful lane the attractive Black Dog & Duck has a part thatched and part tiled roof with brick, timber and plastered walls. In the 1700's the house was owned by a haulier who brought coal from Newcastle to supply the furnaces at Amberley chalk pits. Later it was bought by George Henley. When navvies were working on the nearby railway they came to the house looking for something to drink but only milk was available so his enterprising wife obtained a licence to press and sell her own cider. It was named Ye Olde Special Cider Shop. In 1815 George applied for, and obtained an ale licence. As he often went shooting with his black dog he subsequently changed the name. The main bar has a flag stone floor, a games area and even an old pianola. Two steps take you up into a pretty dining room with a heavily beamed ceiling, timber plastered walls and a large inglenook fireplace. A narrow passage-way leads down to a delightful little bar, similar to the restaurant, with a warm log fire. There are chairs and tables at the side and more on the large area of grass at the back.

The inn is part of Grand Metropolitan very well and efficiently run by the friendly licensees. Three well kept real ales are served by hand pump, Ruddles Best Bitter, King & Barnes Festive and Webster's Yorkshire Bitter.

A good food menu is available seven days a week. Bar snacks include ploughman's, sandwiches, homemade soup, filled potatoes, pizzas, traditional and seafood lasagne and steak and kidney pie. There is more choice in the restaurant with several starters which could include calamaris and smoked haddock fol-lowed by breaded fillet of plaice with prawns and mushrooms or cheese and broccoli filling, salmon in asparagus sauce and grilled swordfish steaks. Also breast of chicken in Port sauce, venison in red wine and veal escalope in a herb sauce plus home carved house glazed ham.

Children are welcome in the saloon bar and restaurant. Dogs in the main bar.

Opening times in the week, which can be flexible are presently from 11 a.m. till 3 p.m. and 6 p.m. till 11 p.m.

Telephone: (01798) 831485.

Village situated off the A29 about 5 miles north from Fontwell.

Approx. distance of walk: 5 miles. OS Map No. 197 TQ 013/135

Park in the back of the inn, in the lane at the front or by the village hall.

A very enjoyable scenic walk through the peaceful villages of Bury and West Burton, along country lanes, bridleways and part of The South Downs Way. The going is mostly easy except for the steep path up Westburton Hill.

1. Cross the road and walk between the cottages, past more houses and down the narrow path to the main road. Cross over and walk up the bank opposite onto the gravel drive. Bear left then right up to a stile, go into the field and straight ahead keeping fairly close to the hedge on the left. On the corner is a stile which takes you up onto a raised path between two wire fences then through trees after which it descends to meet a stile in the valley bottom. In spring and early summer there are many bluebells and garlic smelling ransoms.

2. Go over the stile and straight across to the stile opposite, over the plank bridge and bear right making your way to the stile in the corner of the field. Climb over and head up the field keeping close to the hedge on the right crossing into the adjoining field upon reaching the stile. Follow the hedge line on the left and continue round until you reach the stile beside the gate, it is signed. The path beyond takes you up to the road at West Burton.

3. Turn left, walk down to the road junction at the bottom of the hill then turn right.

Continue ahead towards the cul-de-sac. Ignore the footpath ahead instead take the signed bridleway on the left between two houses. Easy going at first it soon becomes a steep climb up to The South Downs Way. Turn left along the track which descends gradually for some distance to meet the A272 at which point turn right keeping to the grass verge for a few yards then cross the road.

4. Rejoin The South Downs Way and upon reaching the lane turn left. Just before entering the village take the signed footpath on the right, go up the track, through the gate and across the field to leave by a similar gate on the far side. Follow the little path out into the road, cross over and go up the slope to the church of St John The Evangelist. Make your way across the graveyard to the wall at the back, climb over, past the school, out into the lane and turn left. Turn right at the bend, walk up to the stile at the top, go into the field and follow the hedge line across to the stile and along the path back to the inn.

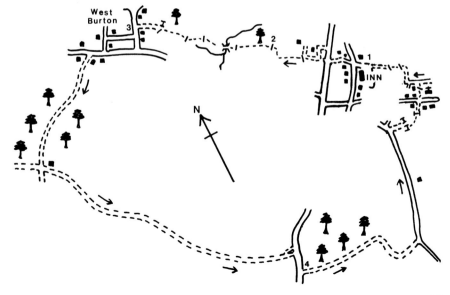

17

The George & Dragon, Burpham

Burpham, pronounced (Burfam) is a lovely Sussex village with a wealth of history and folklore. Arthur Stanley Cooke in his book 'Off The Beaten Track in Sussex' says "seldom is a village so delightfully situated, even in Sussex". The lovely George & Dragon, a stone's throw from the 12th century church, was built in 1736, and started life as an ale house although a pub stood on the site for many years before that. It remained connected with the same family for 350 years. The beautifully kept main bar is comfortably furnished with pine chairs and tables, part of which is on a raised area behind the fireplace. The adjoining low beamed restaurant has some old wood panelling and a large fireplace at one end. There are white chairs and tables outside.

The inn is a free house extremely well run by the tenants James Rose and Kate Holle. An interesting choice of three real ales include Arundel Best, Woodfords Wherry and Hop Back Summer Lightning.

The food is particularly good and available every day except Sunday evening. For just a snack you can have a delicious bowl of homemade soup, pate, ploughman's or one of their lovely sandwiches. Manhattan is chicken, bacon and salad, dressed with mayonnaise in a triple deck and toasted, a meal in itself. Daily specials chalked on the blackboard might include avocado with Selsey crab, duck & black cherry pie, whole mackerel with horseradish and apple sauce, spicy pork with pineapple and ginger plus much more including vegetarian dishes. A separate menu is available in the elegant restaurant including Sunday lunch. Of the many starters you can choose to have fresh scallops - pan fried and served with Pernod and cream and to follow Butterleberli - a Swiss speciality of calves liver, grilled pink, with basil butter. Homemade desserts include boozy cream slice and strawberry cheesecake.

Well behaved children are allowed but only in the restaurant. No dogs inside.

Weekday opening times are 11 a.m. till 2.30 p.m. and 6 p.m. till 11 p.m. Sundays 12 till 3 p.m. and 7 p.m. to 10.30 p.m.

Telephone: (01903) 883131.

Village is close to Arundel reached north from the A27.

Approx. distance of walk: 4¼ miles. OS Map No. 197 TQ 039/089.

Park in the car park behind the pub or in the street at the front.

A lovely downland walk from this delightful village which takes you through Wepham. Although hilly the going is easy underfoot and fairly dry.

1. From the pub walk across the road and up the path to the church. 'St Mary The Virgin' dates from the 12th century, a short history of which can be purchased inside. Bear right across the churchyard to the wall, go up the steps and follow the footpath until it reaches the lane then turn right. At the road junction continue downhill and take the turning on the left.

2. The lane merges with a track and rises gradually towards Perry Hill. Continue through a farm gate until a footpath sign directs you up the hillside. Bear right following the well worn track, through the gate uphill until you meet the fence at the top on Wepham Down. Turn left walking round to join the bridleway and then turn right.

3. Continue straight ahead into the field and down to the bottom keeping fairly close to the fence on the right. After passing through a couple of gates you come to a footpath on the right, it is signed. Go down the bank and over the stile, across the gallop and over a second stile into the field. In spring there are number of cowslips growing nearby.

4. Following the line of the hedge walk up to the top, go over the stile, out onto the track and turn left. Bear right when you reach the lane and walk down to the road junction at Wepham turning right and then first left. As you approach the bend look for a footpath signed up the bank on the left. At the top go over the stile, straight across the field and over the stile on the far side turning right along the side of the playing field back to the pub.

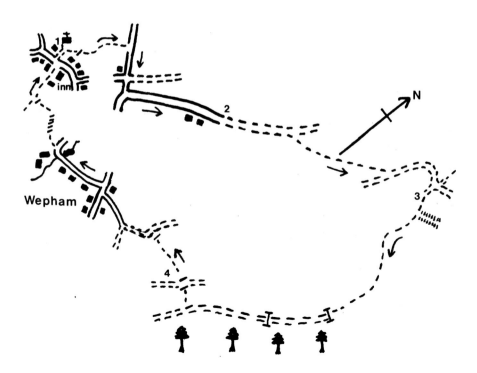

The Black Horse Inn, Byworth

In my opinion no book on Sussex pubs would be complete without the charming, unspoilt Black Horse Inn. The original pub dates from the 14th century but the three story brick front was not added until 1820. The main bar, with its high beamed ceiling and bare wooden floor boards, has simple chairs, tables and padded wall seats and an open coal fire in a large brick fireplace. Three very attractive interconnected rooms, served by the same bar but with an additional fireplace, have plain white painted walls above wood panelling. Furnishings consist of scrubbed pine tables, chairs and wooden pews. A flight of stairs leads up to a delightful Elizabethan restaurant with masses of exposed timbers and yet another open fire. The very attractive, scenic garden has several grassed terraces with picnic benches separated by rows of flowering shrubs.

The inn is a freehouse well run by the owners. There are four real ales, Youngs Bitter, Fullers London Pride, Ballard's Best and Ballard's Golden Bine or Gales HSB.

Seldom have I visited a pub with such an interesting and comprehensive menu that it would be hard not to find a dish to your liking. The food, home cooked on the premises, is served both lunch time and evenings seven days a week. Apart from snacks such as ploughman's a long list of starters include delicious French onion soup, courgettes and prawns au gratin, escargot, langoustines and scallops in garlic. These can be followed by beef bourgignon, shepherds pie, calves liver in sherry, sweet and sour duck with orange, monkfish in cream of mustard sauce - even egg and chips. Each day there are a few specials such as fresh grilled squid and grilled tuna with herbs and rosti.

Well behaved children are welcome and dogs on a lead.

Weekday opening times are from 11 a.m. till 3.p.m. and 6 p.m. till 11 p.m. Sunday 12 noon till 3 p.m. and 7 p.m. till 10.30. p.m.

Telephone: (01798) 342424.

Village signposted from the A283 south east from Petworth.

Approx. distance of walk: 4 miles. OS Map No. 197 SU 987/212.

Park either in the car park at the side or anywhere in the lane at the front.

A most enjoyable walk which takes you along a pretty river path, through the grounds of Petworth House and down an attractive gully once the major turnpike from Chichester to Petworth. It is mostly easy going but can sometimes be a little muddy in places.

1. Leave the inn turning left, and in a short distance but before reaching the main road, go over the stile in the hedge on the left. Walk down to the bottom of the field, through the gap in the hedge and down to the bridge. Cross over climbing the bank to the footpath and turn right. Bear right at the fork and follow the path to the top turning right across to the gate, out onto the gravel track and turn left walking until you reach the road.

2. Cross over, turn left and immediately turn right onto the signed footpath. The scenic path, metalled in places, continues round behind houses. Ignore the paths off to the right but keep walking round until you reach the centre of Petworth then turn right, cross the road and enter Petworth House, signposted Cowyard Footpath. The park is open to the public from 8 a.m. till 9 p.m. or dusk if earlier.

3. Follow the path to the right then left through the tunnel and the iron gates into the park. Bear left to pick up the track which passes beside the lake. Further round leave by the gate house on the left turning right into the A272, and in about fifty yards cross over to the short drive beside the

house and go down the bridleway on the left. It is now a deep gully but was once the old turnpike. Hazel and other trees form a canopy over head whilst ferns and other wild flowers hang down in fronds on either side.

4. Ignore the turnings left and right but continue ahead until you come to the junction of a bridleway then turn left. Walk up to the main road, cross over and continue walking for about half a mile soon to reach a stile on the left opposite the Southern Water Service depot. Bear left down to the stream crossing the stile and follow the path over another stile into a small wood.

5. Leave by the stile and head straight across the meadow, over the wooden bridge in the far corner and follow the path to the right. Bear right when you reach a path junction, cross the stile and continue ahead until once more reaching the bridge near the start of the walk. Go down the bank, cross over and walk up to the gap in the hedge but this time bear half right at the finger post, across the field and up to a small bridge and crossing point behind the pub. Follow the little path uphill, out into the lane turning left back to the pub.

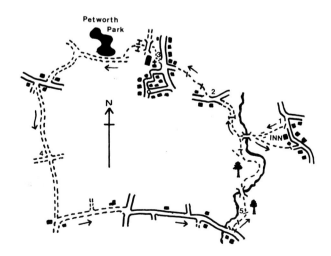

The Charlton Fox, Charlton

This charming 16th century inn was originally called 'The Pig & Whistle' but after the Duke of Richmond made fox hunting popular in the immediate district around Goodwood the pub was re-named 'The Fox Goes Free' but is now known as 'The Charlton Fox'. In November 1915 the first ever meeting in England, and the initiation of The Women's Institute, was held in the back room, now the main bar. The front area of the pub was once a bakery and village shop. The Fox is often mentioned in many of the good pub and guides and justifiably so. From the small porch one enters directly into the cosy snug bar which has a large inglenook fireplace with a warm log fire in winter, a low beamed ceiling and high back wooden settles. The larger bar has a brick floor, part panelled walls as well a large brick fireplace. A large room behind the bar, previously stables, is now a second restaurant and there is seating for up to forty in the delightful restaurant and Old Bakery. At the back is a large lawned beer garden and barbecue area.

This well managed free house can offer a good choice of real ales which presently include Ringwood Old Thumper, Ballards Best and Gales HSB.

Very good home cooked food is available seven days a week. There is a bar menu which includes soup, steak and mushroom pie, chilli, chicken Kiev, curry, large jacket potatoes and generous ploughman's and sandwiches and, at times, fresh crab and lobster salads. Sometimes on the menu is Charlton Hunt pie - a traditional game pie served in a very rich sauce. The restaurant menu is much more comprehensive and includes a selection of vegetarian meals like vegetable lasagne.

Opening times are from 11 a.m. till 3 p.m. and 6 p.m. till 11 p.m. For the summer months the inn usually opens all day on Saturday and Sunday.

Families are welcome and dogs too, if kept under control.

Good accommodation is available.

Telephone: (01243) 811461.

Village signed from the A286 at Singleton.

Approx. distance of walk: 3½ miles. OS Map No. 197 SU 888/130.

Park in the lane at the front.

An enjoyable scenic walk on Levin Down, through Singleton with its Saxon church and back across farm land to the inn. Levin Down is one of the last of the old chalk grasslands and supports a large number of plants and animals. Fortunately the down escaped ploughing and re-seeding and although at one time the area became overgrown volunteers have been helping clear a lot of the dense scrub. The walk is hilly in places but mostly easy going.

1. From the inn turn right towards Singleton, walking past the lane on the right until you reach the stile in the right-hand hedge. Go over and follow the path up the field and over the stile at the top onto Levin Down. Take the path ahead, through the gate and then bear left following the well worn path round the hillside. Keep walking until you reach the stile then follow the path ahead through the woods to the stile and cross into the field turning right.

2. Keeping close to the wire fence, walk to the corner of the field, go over the stile, down to the track and turn left. After rising slightly the track bears right between two fenced fields. Continue for a short distance and, just beyond the corner of the field on the left, look for a bridleway which can become overgrown in summer and easily missed. Turn left here and follow the path back along the opposite side of the field before reaching a farm gate, go through and straight ahead, through a second gate onto the tarred drive.

3. Keep straight ahead past Broadham House and, after passing a pair of cottages on the right, go over the stile into the field on the left. Keeping close to the hedge, walk round until you reach the stile then follow the path up through the woods to the stile at the top. Go into the field and bear left, through the gateway and straight ahead to eventually meet the hedge on the right. When you arrive at the finger post bear left up the field towards the finger post on the bridleway and turn right.

4. Keep walking and then go left across the field by the finger post, over the pair of stiles and down the field, through the gate into the lane turning right towards Singleton. Make a left turn into the lane leading to the Saxon church and then take the narrow path on the left, past the houses in the cul-de-sac and straight ahead between two dwellings, round to a kissing gate and into the field. Cross to the stile on the far side and keep straight ahead following the lane round to the left and back to the pub.

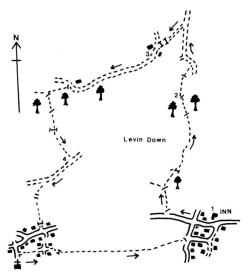

23

The Old House At Home, Chidham

Chidham today is probably still much as it would have been many generations ago - a small peaceful hamlet in an area of unspoilt rural England. The low lying peninsula, jutting out into Chichester Harbour, is home to many seabirds and waders safe in the Nutbourne Marshes Nature Reserve. The delightful 300 year old pub is perfectly in keeping with its surroundings. The lovely interior, although not totally original, still imparts an air of bygone days. The one main bar has a heavily beamed ceiling with timber props. The walls are of wood, brick and plaster construction. At one end there is a small brick open fireplace and at the other a large raised fireplace with a warm log fire in winter. There is a separate area for dining and where families are welcome. Furniture is an assortment of tables, chairs and old settles. There are a couple of picnic benches on the small front terrace and more on the lawn at the back.

The inn is a free house very well run by the owners Terry Brewer and Andy Simpson. The well stocked bars includes four real ales, Ringwood Best Bitter and Old Thumper, Badger Best and Old House Best plus various guests such as Arundel Gold, Gibbs Deacon and Burts VPA.

Very good food, most of it home cooked on the premises, should suit all tastes including vegetarians. There are snacks of ploughman's, jacket potatoes and sandwiches, homemade soup of the day and 'Old House' cream of shell fish soup made with crab, prawns and halibut. As you would expect there are several other sea food dishes including fresh whole plaice, fisherman's pie and Dover sole. Other main course dishes offer a choice of roast beef or turkey, steak & kidney pie, curry, venison, winter rabbit pie, liver and bacon and Selsey crab salad. Each day there is a chef's special such as fresh salmon cutlet - poached in a sherry, white wine and cream sauce.

Dogs are welcome if under control also well behaved children, even muddy boots!

Opening times, Monday to Friday, are from 11.30 a.m. till 2.30 p.m, Saturday 12 noon till 3 p.m, and again from 6 p.m. till 11 p.m., Sunday 12 noon till 3 p.m. and 7 p.m. till 10.30 p.m.

Telephone: (01243) 572477.

Between Emsworth and Chichester turn right from the A259 at Nutbourne by the Barleycorn pub.

Approx. distance of walk: 4½ miles. OS Map No.197 SU 786/040.

Although the inn has its own car park there is ample space in the lane at the front.

A bracing walk ideal for the whole family especially if you are interested in sea birds. It is mostly flat and easy going underfoot. The path follows the shore line round past Cobnor Point and beside the Nutbourne Marshes Nature Reserve. It is one of my favourite walks, a good place to momentarily escape from the fast and furious pace of life today.

1. Turn left from the pub and walk back along the lane, turning left again when you reach a signed footpath on the left between a row of high poplars and a ditch. It runs across fields to meet the shore. The path is then easy to follow needing little or no explanation. It first runs along the top of a raised bank and then along the shore. At Cobnor Point a seat is provided to view the nesting sea birds whilst a notice board gives some useful information about the area and the reserve.

2. After crossing the stile go up the bank. At one point the path diverts behind the sailing club and back to the shore. Keep walking until a signed footpath directs you inland. Go out into the lane and turn right then left at the junction. Look for the signed path on the left then simply follow it round the fields eventually reaching the road opposite the church. Turn left back to the inn.

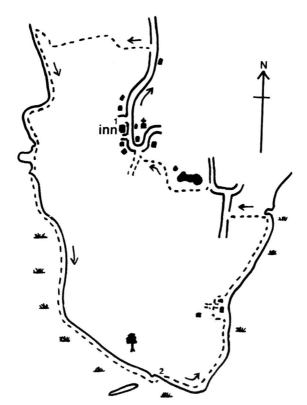

Jack & Jill Inn, Clayton

Clayton is perhaps best known for its two windmills one a smock or post mill the other a tower mill. They have inspired many painters not least Constable who once sketched the tower mill. It is from the two mills that this roadside inn derives its present name. Before that it was known as The Matchfield Arms but originally started life as the village post office. It is an inn with a warm and friendly atmosphere. There are two main bars both comfortably furnished with horse regalia adorning the part wood panelled walls and heated in winter by warm log fires plus a separate family room. Outside there is a beer garden with picnic benches and a large attractive play area for children were there are several farm animals.

The inn is a Phoenix pub now trading as a free house. Real ale lovers will delight in the constantly changing list which presently includes Master Brew and Spitfire from Shepherd Neame, Smiles Bitter plus seasonal beers like Big Fat Santa from the local Brewery On Sea. Food is served seven days a week with a roast on winter Sundays. From the menu, apart from snacks such as ploughman's, pate and soup there is a choice of starters which include three deep fried dishes - crispy cauliflower, garlic courgettes and mushrooms followed by homemade steak & kidney pie, various steaks, breaded chicken fillets, honey roast ham, breaded fish and a vegetarian dish such as spring vegetables in a cheese sauce. There are usually daily specials such as quiche or a curry.

Children are welcome in the family room. Dogs too are allowed if kept on a lead.

Weekday opening times are from 11 a.m. till 2.30 p.m. and 6 p.m. till 11 p.m. Sunday 12 noon till 3 p.m. and 7 p.m. till 10.30 p.m. From April through till September the pub will open for afternoon tea.

Telephone: (01273) 843595.

Pub situated just off the A273 about 6 miles north from Brighton.

Approx. distance of Walk: 5½ miles. OS Map No. 198 TQ 298/143

The pub has its own car park but there is also a parking area at the start of the walk by the sports pavilion.

A fairly long but interesting, scenic walk which takes you past Jack & Jill, the two Clayton Windmills and up onto Wolstonbury Hill, an Iron Age hill fort. The going is fairly easy, mostly dry underfoot but quite steep in places.

1. Leave the pub and cross the road turning right. Make your way over the railway bridge, past the junction with the B2112 then go over the stile onto The South Downs Way, the footpath is signed. Keep to the right-hand side of the playing field towards the pavilion leaving by the metalled road in the bottom right-hand corner. Cross the lane, go over the stile ahead of you, up the track and through the gate towards the windmills. Turn right at the corner of the boundary fence passing through the wooden gate on the right. Jill, a white post mill, is the first windmill you come to and is open to the public.

2. Leave the car park by the metalled road and turn left up the hill taking the right-hand farm track past Jack, a tower mill. Further ahead fork right down to New Barn Farm, go through the gate and continue ahead crossing The South Down Way with the golf course on the right. As you pass close to one of the greens the path drops downhill bearing right. Make your way up to the brow of the hill. On the right is a signed bridleway leading to a five bar gate. The public footpath runs across the golf course then through a gate and down the

hill. Keep to the fence on the right and as you approach Pycombe go to the right of the mound, out though the gate into the road and turn right.

3. After about 50 yards turn left into School Lane, signposted 'South Downs Way'. When you come to the crossroads, but just before reaching the church, turn right onto The Wyshe, a narrow metalled road which becomes a track up through the trees. Keep straight ahead crossing a footpath then over another path junction, through the gate and bear left towards Wolstonbury Hill. Keep walking and when your reach a gate in the hedge walk up to the triangulation point.

4. With your right shoulder facing the windmills go due north looking for the footpath down towards Clayton. It is a steep drop to the valley down a well walked path passing through woods before reaching a bridleway. Ahead of you is a stile beside a gate go through and, fifty yards further on, turn right at the track junction, through a second gate and onto the track across open fields. It narrows before reaching New Way Lane on the other side of a farm gate. Keep straight ahead back to the pub.

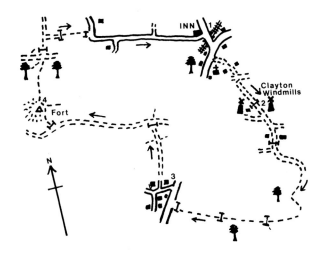

The Hurdlemakers, East Dean

East Dean has been inhabited for centuries. There are Celtic fields at Court Hill above the village and Bronze Age round barrows in the parish. The local people worked on the land, in the forests or for the Duke of Richmond who owned the Manor. Hurdle making was one of the principal trades; before the First World War there were seven hurdlemakers in the village but now there are none. In recognition of their craft the village pub, which dates back to 1755 and known until 1990 as The Star and Garter, was renamed 'The Hurdlemakers' by the new owner Roger Waller. There is one 'locals' bar and a comfortable lounge with part dark wood panelled walls, an open fire and lots of copper pans displayed around the walls. At the back is a covered area with additional seating, a secluded lawned beer garden and the old stables - ideal for small parties, families and walkers.

The inn is a free house serving up to five or six real ales such as Ushers Best, Ballard's Wassial, Adnams and Ruddles Best plus guest ales as well as a selection of country wines or even a pot of tea.

Good home cooked food is available seven days a week with a roast on Sunday. There are snacks of ploughman's, jacket potatoes, homemade soup and toasted sandwiches with tasty fillings like ham and peach or Stilton and tomato. Main course dishes are cooked to order. Supreme of chicken is poached breast dressed on peeled prawns and covered in lobster sauce. Various fish dishes include hot giant prawns and vegetarian meals range from a hot pineapple slice topped with Galliano to vegetable delight - cauliflower, broccoli and asparagus in creamy cheese. Daily specials might offer one marinated braised steak pie in red wine, pan fried lamb with wild mushroom sauce, chicken and pasta shapes in a cream sherry sauce and chef's seafood pie - salmon, trout, codling, cockles, mussels and prawns in a garlic and cheese sauce topped with mashed potato. You can even have fish and chips to take away.

Weekday opening times are from 11 a.m. till 2.45 p.m (Saturday 3 p.m.) and 6 p.m. till 11 p.m. Sunday 12 noon till 3 p.m. and 6.30 p.m. till 10.30 p.m.

Children are welcome away from the bar, dogs also.

Overnight accommodation in stable annexe.

Telephone: (01243) 811318.

The delightful village of East Dean is signed from the A286 at Singleton and also from the A285, Chichester to Petworth road.

Approx. distance of walk: 5 miles. OS Map No 197 SU 905/131.

Park in any of the roads close to the pub.

East Dean, like so many other villages in this delightful area of West Sussex, has remained unspoilt by time. Attractive flint cottages overlook the village green and pond. The walk is extremely enjoyable, not over demanding, mostly through woods, on farm land and through Goodwood Country Park.

1. From the inn turn left, past the green and up the lane towards Goodwood. On the right look for a short track leading up to a gate, the path is signed. Go over the stile into the field and straight ahead up to the stile in the far corner. Bear left up the field making for the stile beside the gate in the top corner. The path ahead is not well defined but try and keep to a straight line until you round the brow of the field where you will see a gate in the left-hand corner, go through and follow the track out to the road.

2. Cross over into Goodwood Country Park and make your way across the green on the left through the picnic area to pick up an attractive fenced, woodland path in the far corner. Cross the stile onto the field then bear right to the stile opposite and go out into the lane. There are two alternatives. Either keep to the road or go over the stile opposite walking beside the hedge. Both routes bring you to a gravel track leading downhill to woods on the left. Follow it round the bends turning left when you meet the bridleway along a narrow strip of woodland.

3. It is a straight track which rises slowly through woodland. There are many wild flowers growing along the path (muddy in winter) which include ragged robin, ox-eye daises and heath spotted orchids. At the top of the clearing the track bears to the left and meets the road. Either go over the stile opposite and across the field to meet the bridleway or turn right walking down the road for a few paces and then left onto the bridleway. After a while take the signed footpath off to the right.

4. Follow it down into the woods until you reach the stile. Walk straight across the field, over the stile opposite and back into the woods. In spring the path is doted with bluebells and primroses. Turn right when the path eventually rejoins the bridleway, go through the gate and down the field keeping close to the boundary. At the bottom descend the bank and turn left along the narrow track then climb the right bank and cross the stile into the field. Walk straight ahead to the stile beside the gate, out into the lane and turn left back to the pub.

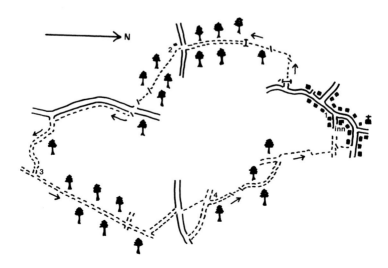

The Three Horseshoes, Elsted

Elsted is an ancient village - its church alone dates back to the time of Edward the Confessor and was built sometime between 1004 and 1066. In 1893 it was destroyed by a tree and became a ruin. Happily it was rebuilt as recently as 1951. The village pub, just a short distance away, itself dates back to the 16th century and was originally built as a drovers' ale house. I doubt if it has changed little since that time. Stepping through the latched front door is a step back in time. Three low beamed rooms have brick or plank floors and form the main part of the pub. At one end is a charming, pine furnished, dining room overlooking the downs. The room next to the dining room has a magnificent inglenook fireplace with a warm log fire in winter. One half of the main bar is divided by old wooden beams and reached down a couple of steps. The furniture is an assortment of old individual tables, chairs and high back wooden settles. Fresh eggs are on sale at the bar and daily newspapers are kept in the rack. There are lots of tables on the sunny back lawn.

The inn has remained a free house and for the past three years has been very well run by the present owner, Andrew Beavis. Real ale is still served traditionally straight from at least five constantly changing barrels behind the bar. Presently there is Ballards Best, London Pride, Cheriton Pots, Ringwood 49er and Hop Back Summer Lightning.

A very good food menu (no chips or sandwiches!), available from 12 noon till 2 p.m. and from 7 p.m. till 9.30 p.m. except Sunday evenings in winter, is chalked on the blackboard in the main bar. A large selection of ploughman's and homemade soup feature on the menu plus homemade steak and Murphys pie, a vegetarian dishes such as broccoli and brie lasagne and aubergine and mozzarella bake, also Selsey crab and lobster in season.

Children are only allowed in the dining room. Dogs on a lead only in the bar and in the garden.

Opening times are from 11 a.m. till 2.30 p.m. and 6 p.m. till 11 p.m. Sunday 12 noon till 3 p.m. and 7 p.m. till 10.30 p.m.

Telephone: (01730) 825746.

Elsted is best reached from the A3 off the B2146 from Petersfield. Continue east through the village of South Harting. Alternatively, if coming from Chichester, take the B2141 off the A286.

Approx. distance of walk: 5¼ miles. OS Map No. 197 SU 818/197.

Apart from the pub's own large car park there is a small area close to the green.

A very enjoyable scenic walk which takes you up onto the South Downs Way and back through Treyford. Most of the walk is on bridleways with the section back to the pub across farm land. The going is fairly steep at times with the surface often very muddy and uneven.

1. Leave the inn and turn left then left again onto the Treyford road. At the bend continue straight ahead along the gravel track towards the downs. The bridleway bears left and then right before entering the woods. Turn right and follow the main track up the rise turning left upon reaching the signed bridleway. Climb the steep path, cross the track and continue ahead to the top.

2. Bear right onto the South Downs Way following the track up the hillside turning left at the junction of another bridleway. Go through the gate and continue ahead onto the tarred drive passing dwellings on the right. Approaching the right-hand bend keep straight ahead, through the small gate and cross the field leaving through the gateway on the far side then turn left onto the bridleway.

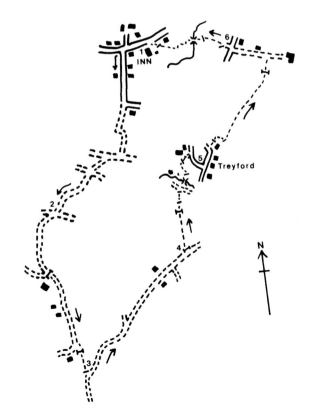

3. Follow the track to the valley bottom and up the other side, ignoring the signed footpath on the left. Continue through Buriton Farm until the track dips towards Treyford. On the left is a gate leading into a field, the footpath is signed.

4. Bearing slightly left walk down the field to a stile and enter the small wood which in spring is carpeted with garlic smelling ramsons. Climb the stile on the far side and walk down the field to the stile at the bottom. Cross the track and continue ahead, over the bridge and the stile, out onto the bridleway and turn left. Further on turn right, go over the stile into the field and walk up to the farm. Cross the stile and make your way to the right of the barn, through the farmyard, out into the lane and turn right.

5. Take the next turning on the left walking past the cottages and continue ahead up the bank, over the stile and follow the path round the field, over another stile into the field and turn left. Keeping close to the hedge on the left, follow the path over three more stiles and across the field to a gate. Make your way over to the farm track, turn left and then right when you reach the lane.

6. Cross the road and go over the stile beside the gate. Bearing slightly right, walk across the field to the stile in the far fence and then cross the small bridge and bear left round the field, into the adjoining field and bear left up to the gap in the far hedge. Go through and continue to the top of the field, over the stile following the little path back to the pub.

An unusual wooden sculpture beside the bridleway at Buriton Farm

Garlic smelling Ransoms carpet the path on a part of the walk

The Sloop Inn, Freshfield Lock

The Sloop, situated by the derelict Ouse Canal, was originally two brick built bargemens' cottages converted in 1815. The name is derived from the sloops (sailing vessels with one mast) which used to work on the river. There are two bars, one has a flag stone floor (ideal for walkers) the other is a more comfortable lounge with armchairs and comfortable sofas. There is seating outside in the tiled porch and more tables and chairs and a childrens' climbing frame in the pretty sheltered garden beside the canal.

The inn is owned by Beards (who have long since ceased brewing their own beer). Harveys Best Bitter and Beards Best are the two regular real ales.

Very good home cooked food is served seven days a week. Apart from the usual pub snacks such as ploughman's and filled jacket potatoes there is a tasty homemade chicken liver pate and delicious homemade soups like cream of smoked salmon, venison with red wine, duck with cranberry and cream of Stilton with celery. Other meals include fried fish and Brighton plaice, Sussex roast ham, Lincoln sausages, salmon steaks, char-grilled chicken and chicken tikka masala also lasagne al forno, smoked salmon and prawn quiche plus 'Dave' sized mixed grill. To follow there is a list of sweets which include bread & butter pudding, pavlova with fresh raspberries and triplet fudge cake with fresh cream.

Weekday opening times are from 11.a.m. till 3 p.m. and 6 p.m. till 11 p.m. Sunday hours can be flexible but generally from 12 noon till 3 p.m. and 7 p.m. till 10 30 p.m.

Children are allowed in both bars but dogs in the public bar only.

Telephone: (01444) 831219.

From Haywards Heath turn off the A272 at Scayne's Hill into Church Road and after about half a mile take the left turn, signed to Freshfield.

Approx. distance of walk: 6 miles. OS Map No.198 TQ 385/243.

The pub has an adequate car park but alternatively there is roadside parking between the pub and the river.

An easy level walk across fields and along country lanes with views of the Bluebell Line.

1. Turn right from the pub over the river bridge and up the road until you reach the stile on the right-hand bend. Cross a couple of stiles into a wood where the path sign points the way over a wooden crossing point into a field. With your back to the pub head for the centre point of a row of trees. Go through the gate, over the bridge and through a second gate into a field. Continue along the right-hand fence over the stile and across to another stile in the bottom corner of the field. Cross the stream and the stile into the field and immediately go left over one more stile into the adjoining field. Make your way up and over the rise towards the finger post leaving by the gate. Cross the road and turn left.

2. Continue ahead at the cross roads, down the hill, under the railway arch and over the river bridge. There is a stile just before the

rail bridge which enables you to climb the bank and if lucky catch sight of a train on the Bluebell Line. When you reach the last of the houses on the double bend continue straight ahead on the track between two farm buildings. Go over the stile beside the gate into the field beyond and down past the brick built hut on the right, then over the stile, down through the wood to meet the road.

3. Cross over and turn left walking past the golf club to the bottom of the hill and over the river bridge. On the right is a signed footpath. Go through the gap in the hedge and follow the path beside the River Ouse. When you eventually reach a footpath junction turn left along a broad track and across to the far boundary. Climb the stile and small bridge and walk across the field leaving by a gap in the hedge turning left onto

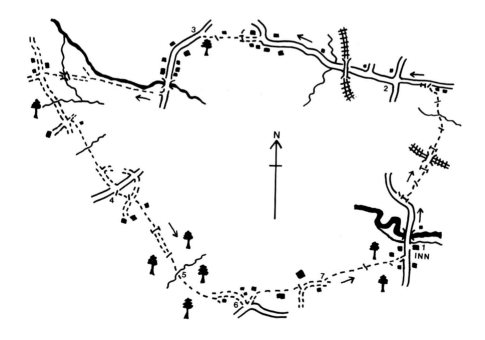

35

the concrete farm road. On the brow of the hill look for the stile beside the farm gate and enter the wood, cross the stream, continue through more woods, across another brook to a metalled track.

4. When you reach the lane walk straight across, over the stile into the field, across to the stile on the far side and out into the road. Cross over and go up the steps to the stile into the field and bear right to a stile beside the gate in the corner. Walk across the drive and down the right-hand side of the garage to the stile in the fence, across the lawn and over the stile into the lane. The stile ahead of you leads onto a track across the field to a stile beside a gate. Cross over and walk to the right of a small tree plantation and straight ahead to the stile into the wood on the far side of the field.

5. Cross the little stream and bear right following the footpath through the woods until you eventually reach the gate turning left onto the track. At the top of the rise turn left onto the track way and continue ahead under the electricity cables and up the rise ignoring the track on the left. Turn left at the next track junction up to the house through an avenue of trees to the right of the house and buildings and through the gate into the lane.

6. Keep straight ahead. Just before reaching the main road turn left into the drive the path is signed. Go to the right of the house, over the stile into the field, and keeping close to the left-hand boundary, walk over to the stile on the far side and then bear diagonally up to the stile in the top corner. Go over onto the path between the hedges, into the field and walk across, through a gateway and bear left to the stile in the far left-hand corner, down the steps to the road and turn left.

7. At the end of the concrete road turn left onto a footpath beside the garage following it into the wood. The path emerges into a field and is signed diagonally down the hill. As you come over the brow turn right by the electricity pole following the fence line to the stile at the bottom far right-hand corner. Go down into the wood bearing left, then left onto another path which leads up to a road ahead. Walk down to the pair of white gates, go through the one on the left into the paddock and bear left to the stile in the far corner, out into the lane back to the pub.

A train on the Bluebell Line

Wakehurst Place, Walk No. 2

Arundel Castle, Walk No. 23

The Shepherd & Dog, Fulking

Tucked away in the South Downs at the western end of the hamlet is the delightful Shepherd & Dog. It dates from the 14th century and was presumably named after the shepherds that farmed on the surrounding downs and would wash their sheep in the Fulking stream. Inside the bar has a partly beamed low ceiling, bare brick and panelled walls and a large inglenook log fireplace surrounded with many copper and brass items. Around the walls are shepherds' crooks and various other old artifacts. The furniture is simple with attractive window seats. There is a childrens' play area at the back of the pub and several grass terraces with a stream running through. There is more seating on the sunny front terrace, a picture in summer with lots of flower tubs and hanging baskets.

The inn is a Phoenix pub presently serving three real ales Harveys Best, Flowers Original and Boddington's Bitter plus a couple of guests.

It is a popular place to eat and looking at the excellent menu one can see why. All the food is homemade and freshly prepared on the premises each day. Lunch time snacks, served between 12 noon and 2 p.m, include a choice of nine different ploughman's alone. The evening menu, served from 7 p.m, offers a wider choice. Starters such as crab mornay, homemade smoked mackerel and spinach roulade and smoked salmon and cream pate are followed by Meg's fresh smoked salmon steak, pork stroganoff, Gerade's famous fillet of plaice stuffed with spinach in a dill and white wine sauce, homemade vegetarian pancakes and Celia's lamb klefftico - shoulder of lamb foil baked with garlic, thyme, rosemary and wine served on a bed of rice. There is also their famous homemade beef and Guinness pie, Nick's lamb kebab en croute and half an oak smoked chicken served hot in a tarragon, mushroom and cream sauce. There are always daily specials on the menu board.

Weekday opening times are from 11 a.m. till 3 p.m. and 6 p.m. till 11 p.m. Saturday 11 a.m. till 11 p.m. and Sunday 12 noon till 10.30 p.m.

Children are not allowed inside the pub but there is no objection to well behaved dogs.

Telephone: (01273) 857382.

The hamlet is situated north of Shoreham-By-Sea close to the border with East Sussex. It can be reached from the A2037 or from the A281. Sussex Bus run a Friday service from Chichester leaving at 8.25 a.m. returning at 1.55 p.m.

Approx. distance of walk: 5 miles. OS Map No.198 TQ 246/115.

Parking is rather limited but there are two lay-bys just before reaching the pub.

An easy walk on country lanes and footpaths with magnificent views from the Devil's Dyke escarpment and ridge.

1. As you face the pub there is a signed bridleway on the left. Go up this path and turn right onto the footpath behind the pub. Cross the stile in the fence at the top and turn left, up the steps and through the trees. Follow the footpath up the escarpment and the hillside ahead on the clearly defined path. When you reach the five finger post sign continue ahead up the track.

2. As you near the ridge go through the gate and follow the footpath round to the left passing the triangulation point and make your way towards the Devils Dyke Hotel. Conveniently open all day it is an ideal refreshment stop. Hang gliding and paragliding takes place from the top.

3. Continue down the main road, ignoring the first two footpaths on the left, and make your way to the top of the hill then turn left onto the track, signposted South Downs Way. Keep straight ahead on the ridge, ignoring the side turnings, until you reach the cross tracks then turn left. The path drops down to a farm gate, continue ahead onto the bridleway and walk down the hill

making for the far end of the valley.

4. At the bottom is a stile beside a gate, pass through and continue ahead along the track until you reach the main road then turn left walk past the rectory and go up the little path into the churchyard. Walk through, out into the road at the front and straight ahead on the Henfield road. It is a busy road but there is a wide grass verge. Turn left when you reach Mill Lane walking along the concrete roadway, past the water works and cross the stile at the end of the lane. Keep to the brook on your left, over the stile beside the gate towards the bridge then cross to the far bank.

5. Continue ahead over the stile beside the gate and walk across the field making for a stile in the right-hand corner. Go into the adjoining field and, keeping to the right-hand hedge, cross the stile beside the gate, go out into the road and turn left. Continue down past Hillbrook Nurseries bearing right at the end of the lane. At the main road keep straight ahead back to the pub.

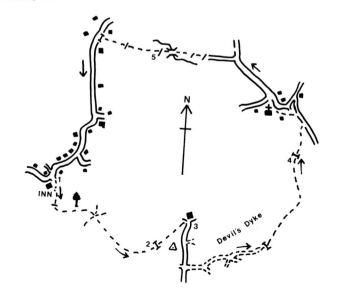

The White Horse, Graffham

The White Horse was originally a small holding and dairy farm then later an ale house. It is a popular village local in an attractive spot with splendid downland views. There is one main bar with an adjoining dining area on a slightly higher level. At the back is a large attractive conservatory restaurant. The simple plain interior has part light wood panelling and comfortable light wooden settles, wooden window seats and furniture. In the bar a large open brick fireplace has a warm log fire in winter. There is a small attractive lawn at the back with white tables and chairs.

The inn is a free house very well run by Roy & Jean Griffith. The well stocked bars include five real ales - four regular beers, Batemans Victory, Palmers Bridport Bitter, Old Speckled Hen and Dorchester Bitter plus a guest such as Abbot Ale.

The White Horse is a popular place to eat offering both a bar and restaurant menu. Served daily from Tuesday till Sunday between noon and 2 p.m. and again from 7 p.m. till 9 p.m. snacks include sandwiches, homemade soups, omelettes, jacket potatoes, ploughman's of cheese or home cooked pate. There are the usual grills, fish dishes and perennial favourites such as steak and kidney pie. The restaurant menu offers a good range of home cooked meals such as pork fillet with cream and mustard, chicken breast with tarragon, beef stroganoff and much more. All vegetables are freshly cooked with a choice of potatoes and there is always a vegetarian dish available.

Children are welcome in the conservatory or the dining room and there is no objection to dogs on a lead.

The inn is closed all day Monday otherwise weekday opening times are from 11 a.m. till 3 p.m. and 6 p.m. till 11 p.m. Sunday from 12 noon till 3 p.m. and 7 p.m. till 10.30 p.m.

Telephone: (01798) 867331.

Peaceful Graffham Village lies about 8½ miles north of Chichester and signed from the A285 and A286.

Approx. distance of walk: 4 miles. OS Map No.197 SU 927/176.

The inn has a substantial car park at the front.

An enjoyable walk, not too long or demanding, but full of interest throughout. At first across farm land to the delightful little hamlet of Upper Norwood, through the Lavington Stud and finally back through downland woods.

1. From the inn turn right, walk down the lane and go up the tarred drive on the left, the path is signed. Pass through the gate at the bottom and bear left, across the field, out through the small gate in the far hedge and follow the little path down across the stream, out into the lane and turn left.

2. Continue up the hill until you reach a footpath on the right signed between two dwellings. Take this path down into a small wooded area, across another path and keep straight ahead, over the stream, through the gate into the field and bear right to the gate on the far side. Go through and bear left, over the rise and down to a stile in the hedge. After negotiating the bank, cross the bridge and bear right following the little path through the small bluebell wood and then beside the field, out into the lane and turn left.

3. A short distance along the lane you come to a stile on the right, go over and bear left walking up the field to the stile in the far hedge, cross onto the path, over a second stile, across the narrow track and keep straight ahead following the wider track down through the trees to the lane at Upper Norwood.

4. Turn right through the hamlet passing on your way some lovely houses looking for a farm track on the right, the path is signed. Go up only as far as the stile on the left, cross both stiles and bear left up and across the field making for the stile to the right of the dwelling. Cross the track and the stile opposite into the field walking until you reach another stile then climb into the adjoining field and turn right crossing the small plank bridge and then the stile onto the bridleway.

5. Head towards the downs, over the cross track keeping straight ahead, past Laving-

ton Stud Farm and out to meet the drive. There are two path options, you can turn immediately right and follow the drive back to the village or take the more scenic path through the trees the only slight disadvantage it can be very muddy and slippery when wet. To continue head across the grass to the stile and make your way left, up the path through the trees to join the bridleway and then turn right.

6. When you eventually reach the track turn right down to the lane, past more attractive houses and the Church of Saint Giles. On the left, opposite Guillods Cottages, is a stile. Go into the field and keeping to the hedge boundary walk round crossing the stile in the hedge, down the dip, over the bridge and stile into the field, up to a couple more stiles and straight ahead across the field to the stile beside the car park and the pub.

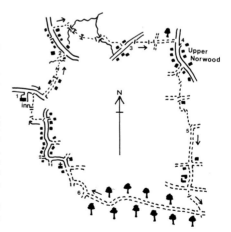

The Unicorn, Heyshott

Although not mentioned in the Domesday Book, burial mounds on top of the downs suggest there were settlements in the area around 1600 B.C. Today Heyshott is no more than a collection of peaceful cottages and farm buildings with the downs to the south and woodland in the north. The Unicorn is a busy country pub situated in a peaceful spot at the foot of the downs. It was originally built as an agricultural cottage around 1843 and not long after became an inn. The one delightful L shaped bar has an enormous inglenook fireplace at one end with built in seats whilst at the other there is an attractive restaurant with glorious views towards the downs. The walls are part brick, beamed and painted, the ceilings heavily beamed. In the carpeted seating areas away from the bar are a number of tables, chairs and comfortable wooden settles. At the back is a sunny beer garden.

The inn is a free house very well run by the owner Maria Simpson offering a selection of real ales which might include Burton Best, Ballards Bitter and Marston's Pedigree plus a guest beer such as Old Baily.

A very good menu, chalked on the blackboard in the bar, is available seven days a week with a roast on Sunday. Apart from the usual snacks of ploughman's and filled rolls there might be salads, home cooked ham, steak and kidney pie and chicken and almond bake. Starters listed on the restaurant menu include garlic mushrooms and Unicorn tossed salad with vinaigrette followed by a tender lamb steak marinated in mint and rosemary, butterfly chicken breast marinated in fruity Cajun seasoning and fillets of sole with crab and scallop filling. Vegetarian dishes might include aubergine lasagne and bruzzoni macaroni, also childrens' meals please ask at the bar.

'Children and dog friendly'.

Weekday opening times are from 11 a.m. till 3 p.m and 7 p.m. till 11 p.m. Sunday 12 noon till 3 p.m. and 7 p.m. till 10.30 p.m.

Telephone: (01730) 813486.

The village is best reached from the A286 about a mile south from Midhurst. Turn right when you reach Heyshott Green.

Approx. distance of walk: 5 miles. OS Map No. 197 SU 899/180.

There is a good sized car park at the side of the pub but it is possible to park safely in the lane at the front.

An extremely enjoyable walk on Heyshott and Graffham Downs. It is fairly steep at times and can be a bit demanding also a little muddy in places during bad weather.

1. Turn left from the inn towards the village and take the lane on the left opposite the church. Walk past the farm and go through the gap into the field on the left making your way up to the distant farm building. (Alternatively you can keep to the lane turning left when you reach the track on the bend). Leave the field through the gap, continue up the track passing the farm building on the left. The path ahead to Heyshott Down is signed up a narrow gully between two fields but has become hopelessly overgrown. Until such time as it might be cleared I suggest you do as all the others and go into the field on the left walking up beside the field boundary until you find a gap on the right and can join the path.

2. The path rises gradually between trees and after passing a field entrance a sign on the right directs you up a narrow winding path through the trees. Although easy to follow it is extremely steep in places and to make things a little more difficult there are several fallen trees lying across the route. At first the path veers to the right before heading left to a meet a stile at the top.

3. Go over into the field and bear slightly left across to join the South Downs Way then turn left. Keep to the main track ignoring all side turnings and paths for just over a mile. Where the track passes through woodland a bridleway forks left, turn here and walk down turning left again when you meet a signed footpath on the left. Near the bottom ignore the path off to the right but continue ahead close to the field boundary.

4. Eventually you will see a gate leading into a field on the right, the path is signed. Go through and keep straight ahead crossing the bridleway, pass through the gate and climb the stile into the farm yard turning left. Almost immediately bear right between the buildings, past the house and up the drive. After passing through the entrance gate immediately go over the stile into the field on the left and bear right over to the wooden crossing point in the hedge. Go into the field and keep straight ahead to pick up a grass track on the far side. It merges with a gravel track and passes Manor Farm before reaching the lane. Take the lane ahead back to the pub.

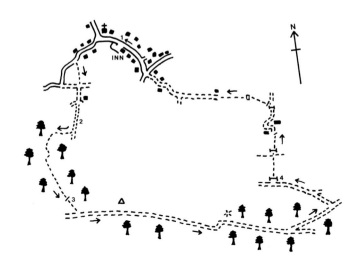

The Royal Oak, Hooksway

Throughout West Sussex there are many isolated country pubs, generations old and happily still unspoilt by the 20th century. The Royal Oak is one of them. Nestling peacefully under the downs at the end of a quiet country lane it is in perfect walking country. This cottage inn dates back to the 15th century and for over 300 years was simply an ale house. Among its more famous patrons over the years have been no less than three kings, Edward VII, George V and King Alfonso of Spain. There are two bars simply furnished with brick and stone floors each with an open fireplace. To the side of the main bar is a small games room and across the car park the delightful 'Hideaway Restaurant'. There are wooden benches and tables on the sunny front lawn, more tables and chairs and a barbecue at the side and a childrens' wooden play fort at the back.

The inn is a free house offering a choice of at least five real ales which can include Bishop's Tipple, Wiltshire Pendragon, Deacon, Wake Ale, Salisbury and Morland Old Speckled Hen.

Bar meals include snacks of filled jacket potatoes and ploughman's plus a good selection of homemade dishes like steak and kidney pie, chilli and the inn's speciality, local venison pie plus at least one vegetarian dish. The restaurant is open from 7 p.m. till 10 p.m, Tuesday till Saturday evening and Sunday lunch time. There is an interesting choice of food which could include baked stuffed mushrooms with a filling of chopped sausage and mozzarella cheese and a hot quiche of leeks with Roquefort cheese served with a celery sauce. The main menu which offers three vegetarian dishes also has a good selection of game such as jugged hare and breast of wood pigeon. Fish dishes include whole Dover sole and monk fish in parcels of filo pastry served with a saffron sauce.

Both children and dogs are welcome.

Normal opening times are from 11 30 a.m. till 2 30 p.m. (12 noon till 3 p.m. Sunday) and 6 p.m till 11 p.m. (7 p.m. till 10.30 p.m. Sunday) The inn is closed on Mondays. Afternoon cream teas are served in the summer.

Telephone: (01243) 535257.

Hooksway is signed from the B2141 midway between Petersfield and Chichester.

Approx. distance of walk: 3¼ miles. OS Map No. 197 SU 815/163

Park at the pub or in the lane.

A short but enjoyable walk mostly through peaceful woodland. It is ideal for families being completely away from any busy roads.

1. Leave the pub and turn left walking just a short distance up the gravel track then turn immediately right towards the gates and take the signed footpath on the left up into Phillis Wood. Sadly many of the trees were brought down in the hurricane of 89 and several still lay across the path, hopefully they will soon be removed. After a while the footpath is signed away from the track and up a bank on the left. Follow it through the trees until you reach a gate, go through and keep straight ahead close to the hedge on the left.

2. Pass through the gate in the corner and walk along the field boundary to the stile then bear right down the field in the direction of the barn. Just before reaching the bottom there is a rough track, turn right and follow it back up the hill to a farm gate. Go through into a woodland strip and continue ahead until it eventually merges with a tarred drive, turning right when you reach the lane.

3. Follow the lane round for about a quarter of a mile turning right at the road junction and take the footpath on the left signposted before the entrance to the West Dean Estate. Amongst the many wild flowers growing along the path are clumps of giant bellflowers. At the stile cross into the field and walk down to the corner, over another stile and bear left following the hedge round to one more stile. Take the rough grass track ahead, crossing the track into the woods, over a second track following the path down to a stile and onto the bridleway turning right back to the pub.

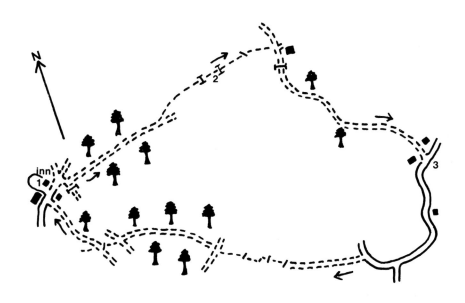

The sketch maps in this book are not necessarily to scale but have been drawn to show the maximum amount of detail.

The Lickfold Inn, Lickfold

Although Lickfold is a tiny hamlet with a population of less than 100 people it is well served with a delightful pub. The lovely Elizabethan inn is of timber framed construction set with herring bone brickwork. Built in 1460 as a coaching inn it was then known as The Three Horseshoes. During 1972 the inn was lovingly restored and renamed. The attractive un-spoilt bar has dark wood panelled walls, a heavily beamed ceiling and a rug on the red brick floor. Hanging from the very large brick inglenook fireplace, which houses a roaring log winter fire, are many old interesting kitchen items. There is a larger seating area on the other side in front of another large fireplace. Other furnishings consist of an assortment of old chairs, tables and high back wooden settles. Many pubs have attractive beer gardens but I think one would have to look a long way to find a nicer one than here. There are eleven separate seating areas on six different levels separated by colourful swathes of flowering shrubs and perennials. There is also as a barbecue.

The inn is a free house well run by the owners Ron and Kath Chambers. The well stocked bar has a very good range of well conditioned real ales which might include Adnams Bitter, Hall & Woodhouse Badger Bitter, Ballards Best Bitter, Draught Bass, Hook Nortons Old Hookey, Fullers London Pride and E.S.B.

The very good food menu, which changes daily, is chalked on the blackboard in the main bar. Weekday lunch time snacks include a delicious choice of filled jacket potatoes, sandwiches and ham with French fries. At other times you can choose starters such as baked avocado, tasty homemade soup, and oriental prawns with chilli, followed by lasagne, roast leg of lamb, chicken curry, steak & mushroom pie, an old fashioned oxtail stew and chicken, broccoli and blue cheese pie. A good choice of fresh dishes might include poached halibut with prawns in white wine, whole plaice, seafood thermidor, lemon sole fillets and poached salmon with a hollandaise sauce.

Children are not allowed inside the pub.

Weekday opening times are from 11 a.m. till 2.30 p.m. (3 on Saturday) and in the evening from 6.30 p.m. till 11 p.m.

Telephone: (01798) 861285.

The tiny hamlet of Lickfold can be reached either from the A286 north of Midhurst, the A283 north of Petworth or from the A272 at Halfway Bridge between Easebourne and Petworth.

Approx. distance of walk: 4½ miles. OS Map No. 197 SU 927/263.

The inn has a small car park at the front and another area at the back. The lane at the front is only just wide enough to park in a couple of places.

A lovely walk much of which is on bridleways through woodland with a small section across farm land and along country lanes. Be prepared though for it to be muddy.

1. Turn left from the pub and take the road towards Fernhurst. After passing Hoewyck Farm the road bears right. On the left is a gate, go through into the field walking down to the bottom, cross the plank bridge, reach the finger post and bear left towards the trees. Drop down the bank and make your way to the stile in the far hedge. Cross the river and go through the gate, straight across the field to the gate opposite, over the plank bridge and follow the path ahead. In summer it does become a little overgrown.
2. When you reach the bridge cross the river and keep straight ahead in the direction of the finger post. It is a grass track, fairly wide in places, which follows close to the stream on the right. The path then heads up a bank to a stile. Turn right down the tarred drive, through the gates and immediately go up the bridleway on the left. After a muddy start the track becomes drier as it climbs steadily through woodland. Ignore the path on the left but keep straight ahead, past two large houses on the left after which the track becomes uneven and muddy as it rises steadily to meet the lane at Bexleyhill.
3. Turn left walking downhill until you

reach a finger post on the right, just beyond the tarred drive. Follow the path along the bank towards the house, down onto the drive and turn right. It is a wide track which passes through mixed woodland. Just before reaching a tile hung house turn left onto the signed bridleway. At first the track descends through woodland (can be very muddy) then beside a clearing after which it joins with a track from the right. Turn right here then right again onto a smaller track, past the house, out into the lane and turn left.
4. If in urgent need of refreshment keep to the road which will bring you back to the pub otherwise after passing the houses cross the stile and join the signed footpath on the right. Make your way across to the finger post keeping straight ahead, over the stile in the fence towards the stile in the far corner. Go over and turn right, walking round the field, over the stile and turn left. Upon reaching the gate on the left go through and turn right, up to the stile and straight ahead, through the gap in the corner of the field, round to a stile and then follow the little path down the bank to the pub.

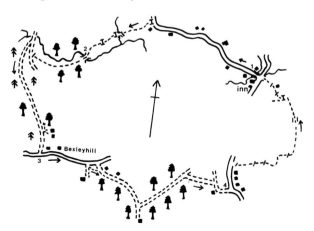

The Hollist Arms, Lodsworth

The Hollist Arms, named after a local family, is a delightful pub in an attractive village setting. There is a small green at the front with seating around a large horse chestnut tree. Up until 1825 the pub was two cottages, in one of them worked the village blacksmith. There is a small bar and restaurant with a massive open brick fireplace, a recently restored snug having an ancient inglenook fireplace and a games and family room also with an open fire in winter. Outside at the back there is an attractive raised beer garden with a barbecue area.

The inn is a free house well run by the proprietors Nicholas Kennard and Sally Turner. A good choice of drinks include up to six gravity fed real ales such as King & Barnes Sussex Bitter, Ballards Bitter plus beers from the Hop Back Brewery, Hall & Woodhouse and Gales.

Very good home cooked food is available seven days a week between 12 noon and 2.30 p.m. and from 7 p.m. till 9.30 p.m. with a traditional roast on Sunday. Bar snacks are listed on the blackboard and include jacket potatoes, smoked salmon, half a dozen crevettes in garlic butter, their own steak and kidney pie and prize winning sausages from a local Chiddingfold butcher. Tasty homemade soups and casseroles are served from cauldrons on trivets by the fireside. The set restaurant menu is more comprehensive and includes chicken dishes, stewed rabbit with lentils, liver and bacon casserole, roast pheasant with Port and bouillabaisse. The Pub's speciality is a locally caught 2lb trout cooked with a creamy butter lemon sauce - sufficient for two people.

The inn is open in the week from 11 a.m. till 3 p.m. and 6 p.m till 11 p.m. Sunday 12 noon till 3 p.m. and 7 p.m. till 10.30 p.m.

Children are welcome in the restaurant or the family room and there is no objection to dogs.

Telephone: (01795) 861310.

Hamlet signed from the A272 at Halfway Bridge between Midhurst and Petworth.

Approx. distance of walk: 3¾ miles. OS Map No.197 SU 928/231.

There is ample parking both at the pub and in the surrounding lanes.

An enjoyable walk ideal for all the family on bridleways through woodland, across farm land and through Cowdray Park.

1. As you face the pub go up the lane on the left and take the next turning on the right. Bear left at the fork and, a short distance up the hill, turn left onto the signed bridleway. It is a wide gravel track passing through an area of coppiced chestnut trees. Ignore the turning to the right but keep going until you reach the house and then turn right onto the grass track. At the end of the wall climb the bank on the left, go over the stile and wooden crossing point, into the field and straight ahead keeping close to the hedge until you meet the track.

2. Walk down to a crossing point, ignoring the left and right turns, and continue ahead between the two fields until the finger post directs you into the field on the left. Keeping close to the hedge walk down to the stile at the bottom, cross into the field on the right walking round the house, out onto the tarred drive and turn right.

3. When you reach the lane turn left. After passing The Holytree Inn, a good halfway refreshment stop, you come to a footpath on the left. Go up between the houses, through the gate and straight across the field to the gate in the far fence. Turn left along the avenue of trees then turn right through the gate and head up the field bearing slightly left to the gate in the top hedge.

4. Follow the path up through the trees and across the golf course taking care to avoid any stray balls. Keep to the track following the signs until you reach a small wooden shelter with a tiled roof then turn left across the green to pick up a path down through the trees. Bear right at the finger post keeping to the grass track leading down to a gate on the left, go through and, keeping to the right of the lily pond, head up and across the park then down to a stile beside a gate on the far side.

5. Go over into the field ahead and turn left walking round close to the boundary, through into another field and turn immediately right. Walk up beside the hedge, through the gap in the corner, out onto bridleway and turn left. Take the right fork up through the woods, turning left into the lane then right at the road junction down the lane to the pub.

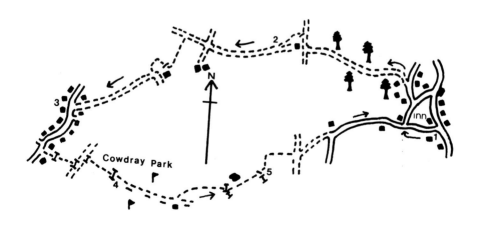

The sketch maps in this book are not necessarily to scale but have been drawn to show the maximum amount of detail.

Noahs Ark Inn, Lurgashall

If having arrived at the pub for the first time you have that feeling of 'deja vu' it might just be because you have seen it on television. Not surprisingly it has been featured many times in advertisements. Few pubs have such a unique village setting overlooking the village cricket green. No one is quite sure about the origin of the name but as a pond once reached almost to the front door this was the most likely explanation. This lovely old brick inn, which looks a picture in summer with the many hanging baskets and flower tubs, dates back to the fourteenth century a fact which becomes obvious once inside. There are two main bars. The simply furnished but comfortable lounge has a part wood block and carpeted floor, a heavily beamed ceiling and an enormous inglenook fireplace with built-in seats and a warm log fire in winter. Similar but larger the Ark Bar has a fireplace at each end. There is a separate cosy dining room and a small family room. All around the walls are many sporting prints and cricket memorabilia. Outside there are tables adjoining the village green.

It is a Greene King tenancy stocking three real ales which presently are IPA, Abbot Ale and Rayments Special Bitter.

Listed in the Good Pub Guide bar food is available every day except Sunday evening between 12 noon and 2 p.m. and 7 p.m. and 10 p.m. The menu includes snacks such as ploughman's and sandwiches, both plain and toasted and home-made soup. Also there are English lamb cutlets, steak and kidney pudding, calves liver and bacon, vegetable chilli and tomato and vegetable tagliatelle. The larger restaurant menu includes escargots and lobster bisque with brandy followed by grilled duck a l'orange, poached salmon in asparagus sauce, venison in red wine and chicken breast with a leek and Stilton sauce.

Children and dogs are welcome.

Weekday opening times are from 11.30 a.m. till 3 p.m. and 6 p.m. till 11 p.m. Sunday 12 noon till 3 p.m. and. 7 p.m. till 10.30 p.m.

Telephone: (01428) 707346.

Lurgashall is in the north of the county and easily reached from the A283, Petworth to Godalming road or from the A286 Midhurst to Haslemere road.

Approx. distance of walk: 4 miles. OS Map No 197 TQ 937/273.

Park where you can in any of the lanes by the green.

A delightful walk in a delightful area from a delightful pub. It is scenic in parts, fairly easy going mostly across farm land, along bridleways and through woods.

1. Leave the pub and go through the small gate down to the church of St Laurence. Saxon in origin it is open daily and well worth a visit. Bear left across the graveyard to the pair of stiles, enter the field and head straight across leaving by the gate on the far side. Bear left and then immediately right onto the track between the ponds. Follow it round to the left, past farm buildings and then to the right entering a wooded area. Cross the bridge and immediately go left over the stile into the field.

2. Keeping close to the hedge on the left, make your way across to the gate in the far hedge, go through and bear right, over the rise to the stile beside the gate in the opposite hedge. Head up the field bearing left at the boundary fence, round to the stile and follow the little path through the trees behind the cottages, out into the lane and turn right.

3. Take the next turning on the left. After passing the farm building you will see a short grass track leading up to a gate on the left. Turn here but do not go through the gate instead take the narrow bridle path on the left. It rises for some distance and then descends to meet the lane. Turn right, walk up the hill and then go left onto the track just before the bend, the path is signed.

Continue ahead (ignoring the signed path down to the left) until you reach a gravel road which takes you past dwellings and out into the lane.

4. Keep straight ahead over the rise and down to the gate way on the left. Go through the squeeze stile beside the cattle grid and walk down through the farm keeping to the main drive. After passing several buildings the track bears right down to a cattle grid but the defined footpath is signed across the grass in front of the converted barn. Walk over to the gate, go through and turn left walking down the drive. Just past the gate house join the little path on the left and follow it through the trees, out into the lane on the far side, turn right and then take the drive on the left.

5. Just before the drive bears right and enters a works yard a footpath leads off to the left through the trees, it is signed. Take this path which joins with a wider track and keep walking until you reach a path junction then bear left, go over the stile and follow the path up into the bluebell wood. Leave by the stile and follow the path across the field keeping close to the hedge on the right, round past the dwelling, into the lane and turn left back to the pub.

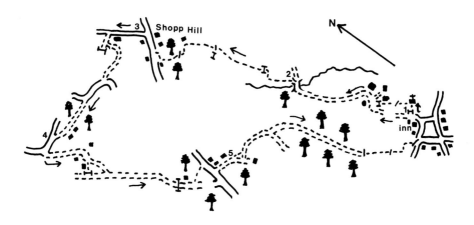

The Black Horse, Nuthurst

This attractive 17th century inn is in a delightful sheltered spot occupying three cottages in what was once a row of five. The simply furnished main bar has a black beamed ceiling, bare brick walls and large flags in front of the enormous inglenook fireplace where a warm log fire burns on cold winter days. A small passageway at the side leads through to a second, carpeted Tudor style snug beyond which is a cosy dining room with a small corner fireplace. At the back a small stone bridge crosses a deeply cut stream to reach a delightful secluded lawn with lots of picnic benches but the most sought after seats are on the sunny front terrace.

The inn is a free house well run by the owners Trevor and Karen Jones. Thomas Hardy Country Bitter is normally available plus up to 20 more at regular beer festivals held all bank holiday weekends.

A good range of bar snacks include basket meals, homemade soup, farm style ploughman's, doorstep sandwiches, stuffed breaded mushrooms and prawn brochettes. Also longboat potato shells - deep fried until crispy and topped with chilli and a lamb balti curry. There are several pies like traditional steak and kidney, chicken, gammon and mushroom and leek also mushroom crepes, chicken tobago, seafood lasagne and homemade cannelloni romagna - spinach, Ricotta cheese, parsley, garlic and Pecorino cheese coated in a creamy tomato sauce with nutmeg and topped with Parmesan cheese. Children have their own menu. A reduced price pasta menu is available on 'Monday Madness' night whilst Friday night is Mexican night.

Weekday opening times are from 11 a.m. till 3 p.m. and 6 p.m. till 11 p.m. Sunday 12 noon till 3 p.m. and 7 p.m. till 10.30 p.m.

Children allowed in dining room only, dogs permitted if under control.

Telephone: (01403) 891272.

Village signposted off the A281 south east of Horsham at Monks Gate.

Approx. distance of walk: 4 Miles. OS Map No. 187 TQ 193/263

Parking is limited at the pub although there are lay-bys in the road.

An enjoyable, easy going walk mostly through woods and across farm land.

1. Turn left from the pub, walk up the hill and take the first turning on the left, the bridleway is signed. Make your way up past the nursery forking left at the top and then turn right onto the bridleway. Go up the drive, through the yard, out onto the track taking the left fork. Make your way up the track turning right before you reach the gate, go past a hay barn and under the high voltage cables. Keep walking ahead until you reach a five way junction and then take the left fork, ignore the immediate path on the left.

2. The track climbs steadily through woods. On the brow of the hill bear left then right keeping straight ahead. Walk down the hill through the woods and, after about fifty yards, turn right onto the track. After a couple of hundred yards turn left onto another track, cross the stream and turn right through the woods keeping the stream on your right. In fifty yards take the left track up through the woods. Ignore the path on the right but keep straight ahead up towards the brow. Continue straight ahead at the footpath sign towards the houses. Cross the stile in the bottom left-hand corner of the field and follow the path out into the road and turn right.

3. Cross over and go down the track on the right-hand side of the black and white house, over the stile beside the gate, into the field and up to the stile in the top right-hand corner. Continue ahead crossing one more stile turning left onto the track. Ignoring the paths left and right, pass under the high voltage cables and up the rise. When you eventually reach the junction turn left onto the metalled road walking through Sedge-wick Park. Take the next track on the left, pass through the gates, go down through the woods leaving by the gate onto the metalled road back to the pub.

The Black Rabbit, Offham

This tranquil riverside inn is a popular spot for the many walkers and tourists visiting Arundel Castle and the nearby Wildfowl & Wetland Trust. John Oliver was the first recorded licensee in 1804 and at that time was popularised by men building the new railway and digging the new cut of the River Arun. Later it became a fashionable watering hole for the Edwardians; even today it still has the outward appearance of an elegant riverside summerhouse. The one long bar has a boarded floor, a warm fire in one end wall and a games area the other. A small adjoining room doubles as a family room. What were once probably the old boat sheds is now the 'Boathouse' restaurant. Seating is provided outside under the verandah and picnic benches are positioned on the terrace beside the river with boat trips available in summer.

The inn is owned by Hall & Woodhouse and very well run by the licensees. Seven real ales presently available are Badger Best, Tanglefoot, Hardtackle, Reg's Tipple, Black Adder, Gribble Ale, and Plucking Pheasant.

A very good and imaginative food menu is available seven days a week with a roast on Sunday. Starters, available as 'lite bites' if preferred, include filled jacket potatoes, homemade soup, potato skins, garlic mushrooms, Cajun chicken and asparagus with main courses such as a vegetable stir fry, gammon steak and a pie of the day. Other dishes include scrumpy pork, cannelloni verdi, rack of ribs, Highland smokies, Cajun swordfish, a mixed grill and Hawaiian chicken. A separate childrens' menu is available and there is a choice of afternoon teas. A special menu is available on Friday evening and a dinner dance at weekends. Sweets include banoffi pie - banana cake on a biscuit base with lashings of cream.

Families are welcome as are dogs.

Weekday opening times are from 11 a.m. till 11 p.m. Sunday 12 noon till 10.30 p.m., with food served between 12 noon and 10.30 p.m.

Telephone: (01903) 882828.

Enter Arundel from the A27 and take the road to the castle entrance. The inn is further along the road just past the wildfowl reserve.

Approx. distance of walk: 5¼ miles. OS Map No. 197 TQ 025/085.

There is plenty of parking both in the inn's own large car park, in the lane at the front or on open ground just before reaching the pub.

Arundel is an historic town its two major attractions being Arundel Castle and The Wildfowl & Wetlands Trust. This lovely and interesting walk is ideal for the whole family. At first it follows the course of the Arun River along a raised bank to the small hamlet of South Stoke. From there it takes you through woods then steeply up onto the downs before descending past Swanbourne Lake and back to the pub between the river and the wildfowl reserve.

1. Walk down across the car park to pick up the footpath in the corner. A narrow path through the trees leads to a stile which allows access to the river path. The raised bank was built to ensure livestock would not be marooned during times of flooding. Wild flowers abound along both river banks in particular large clumps of marsh marigolds. Follow the path across a track by the bridge, through a couple of gates turning left when you reach the hamlet of South Stoke.

2. South Stoke is recorded in the Domesday Book of 1085-86. St Leonard's Church dates from the 11th century and the first cottage No.38 was once an inn. Walk on round and after passing South Stoke farm turn right onto the bridleway. Make a left turn left at the barn and keep to the edge of the field crossing the stile at the bottom into the field and bear right. Keeping close to the fence, walk round then over the stile entering woods on the far side.

3. There are plenty of primroses and vast swathes of ramsons. If you like the smell of garlic then walk in the spring, it is delightful. The path follows close to a wall on the left. When you reach a signed gap go through and follow the path, over a stile and up the hill bearing right at the track and then left. It is a fairly steep climb to the stile at the top. Go over and bear right towards the corner of the small wood following the track round until a path sign directs you off to the right. Follow a line fairly close to the fence, over a wooden crossing point, join the track at the bottom and turn left.

4. Keep to the track along the valley unless of course you want to walk through Arundel in which case continue ahead up the track towards the tower. Arriving at the lake you have two route options, the left path is perhaps the better. Having reached the road walk straight across through to the little path beside the reserve and turn right. Bear left at the bridge then simply follow the path round the reserve then along the river bank back to the pub.

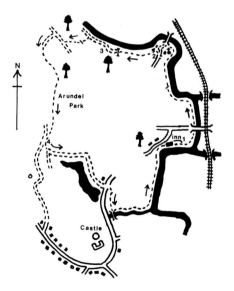

The sketch maps in this book are not necessarily to scale but have been drawn to show the maximum amount of detail.

The Gribble Inn, Oving

Without doubt the Gribble at Oving must surely be one of the most attractive pubs in the county. For many years it was just a private cottage lived in by a Miss Rose Gribble but in 1980 a local farmer was successfully granted a licence, and the inn opened as a free house. In 1987 the lease was bought by the Dorset brewers, Hall & Woodhouse. Throughout this lovely old inn are low, heavily beamed ceilings and timbered bare brick and plastered walls. The main open plan bar is dominated at one end by a large brick inglenook fireplace with a warm log fire set on a raised hearth. A separate, similar dining area also has an open brick fireplace in one corner, wooden settles around the walls and comfortable farmhouse tables and chairs. There is also has a skittle alley. A delightful cottage garden has wooden benches and tables on the grass under the apple trees.

The pub now brews its own beers on the premises which presently include Ewe Brew, Plucking Pheasant, Black Adder II, Pig's Ear, Gribble Ale, Reg's Tipple and Wobbler.

A good food menu is served seven days a week except Sunday evening between 12 noon and 2 p.m. and from 6.30 p.m. till 9 p.m. and is supplemented daily with blackboard specials. There are the usual pub snacks such as salads, ploughman's, freshly cut sandwiches and toasties plus several starters which include locally made smoked trout pate, whitebait and smoked mackerel fillet, followed by various steaks, gammon, Gribble grill and a selection of homemade pies - steak & mushroom and turkey and ham to name but two. Specials dishes could include sausage and apple pie, nut and mushroom fettuccine with salad, chicken Kiev and home made cheese and broccoli quiche.

Children are welcome in the dining area.

Weekday opening times are from 11 a.m. till 2.30 p.m. and 6 p.m. till 11 p.m.

Telephone: (01243) 786893.

The small village of Oving is signed from the A27 east of Chichester and then from the B2144.

Approx. distance of walk: 4 miles. OS Map No. 197 SU 902/050.

The inn has a large car park at the back but you can also park safely in the lane at the front.

Whilst there are few public footpaths in the area surrounding the pub I never the less wanted to include the delightful Gribble Inn in this book. For this reason it does mean a lot of the walk is along the highway, and whilst most of the lanes are very quiet and peaceful care should be taken for the first half mile; although a minor road it can sometimes be busy. I found the section across the farm land was rather overgrown in July and took more time than usual to locate the path. Other than that it is an easy, mostly dry level walk.

1. Turn left from the inn back to the road junction and left again. After about half a mile take the turning on the right, cross the bridge and turn left at the bottom of the hill towards the level crossing at Woodhorn. Carefully cross the track and, just past the entrance to the dwelling, go over the stile in the hedge on the right, cross to the farm gate, enter the field and keep straight ahead walking close to the hedge on the right.

2. Go over the stile in the far corner and, still keeping close to the hedge, make your way across the field until you reach the ditch on the far side and then bear left. Keep close to the ditch for a couple of hundred yards looking for a crossing point, it can become very overgrown in summer. Cross into the field and bear left making your way over to the corner where a plank bridge allows easy access to the field ahead.

3. Walk beside the boundary, past the derelict house on the left and straight ahead into the field in the direction of the finger post.

Follow the left-hand boundary until you reach a farm track through a gap in the corner. Cross over and keep straight ahead down the narrow field to the plank bridge, climb the stile and bear left, up and across the field to the stile beside the gate, out into the lane and turn right.

4. After a short distance turn left at the crossroads on the road to Aldingbourne. Walk through the village forking left at the junction onto the disused airfield. Bear right in the direction of the finger post and then left following the runway. I was last here in 1991 and noticed some areas of concrete were being lifted but have no doubt that the present route of the path will remain and be well signed. Cross another runway and bear left at the next, over to the stile beside the gate, out into the lane and turn right. Keep to the lane for about a mile ignoring the side turnings until the lane eventually bears left back to the pub.

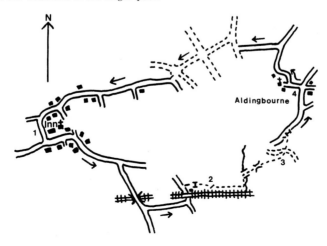

The Royal Oak, Rusper

The Royal Oak at Rusper dates from the 16th century; the two outside extensions were not added till very much later, probably at the time when the railway was built and were used for storage. There are two bars both with beamed ceilings and carpeted floors and heated in winter by an open log fire. Outside there are seats under the glass canopy, on the side patio where there is a fountain and more seats on the lawn at the back. There is also a childrens' play area with old fashioned swings, creasy pole and low beam bars.

The inn is a King & Barnes pub serving their range of well conditioned real ales. Drawn from the cellar there is at present Sussex Bitter, Festive, Wealdman and Broadwood plus occasional guest ales.

All the food, served between 12 noon and 2.30 p.m. and from 7.30 p.m. till 9.30 p.m, is homemade. Apart from the usual snacks of sandwiches, ploughman's and filled jacket potatoes the pub's speciality is bubble & squeak. It comes in four different ways, 'Highland' has added sausage and bacon and the vegetarian version mushrooms and cheese. There is also soup, cottage pie, beef casserole, barbecue spare ribs, home cooked ham, salads, omelettes and good old favourites like liver and bacon, sausage and mash, steak and kidney pie and a vegetarian dish such as vegetable lasagne. A separate evening menu offers more choice. Deep fried Camembert or sardines in garlic butter might be followed by various steaks, mixed grill, chicken breast with a leek and asparagus sauce, venison and fish dishes of lemon sole, swordfish and a seafood platter. And to complete your meal plum crumble and banana split.

Weekday opening times are from 11 a.m. till 3 p.m. and 6 p.m. till 11 p.m. Sunday 12 noon till 3 p.m. and 7 p.m. till 10.30 p.m.

Children and dogs are equally welcome both outside and in.

Telephone: (01293) 871393.

North from Horsham, turn off the A24 just past Warnham. Alternatively take the road to Langhurst at Clark's Green.

Approx. distance of walk: 5 miles. OS Map No. 187 TQ 186/369.

Parking is limited but south of the pub there are areas where it is possible to park in the lane.

An easy country walk on well defined paths, through woods and on farm land. It is fairly dry underfoot and suitable for the whole family but can become muddy in extreme conditions.

1. Leave the pub and turn right and in thirty yards turn right onto the Sussex Border Path, cross the plank bridge and stile through the woods then across the field to the stile on the far side into the field beyond. Bear half left across to the gap in the hedge, go out onto the track and turn half left then go through the gate into the field. About two thirds of the way down look for the stile in the hedge, go through and walk down to the stile in the bottom corner, over into woods forking left. Continue up the rise taking the path on the right.

2. After crossing two bridges the path rises to a stile. Go over into the field and, keeping close to the woods on the right, walk to the stile on the far side. In ten yards turn left, go through the woods, down to the valley bot- tom, cross over the bridge and up the hill- side ignoring the wide track to the left. On the brow of the hill turn left at the cross tracks onto a broad track through open forest. When you reach the stile cross into the field ahead walking uphill towards the tree on the horizon and make for the stile to the left of the brick and tiled house. Follow the boundary of the sports ground turning right before the main road along the foot- path to the church.

3. Continue down the high street taking the left fork towards Crawley then go through to the back of the car park of the Star public house to rejoin the footpath. Walk down behind the houses then over the stile onto the signed footpath. Continue ahead pass- ing through a couple of gates and walk

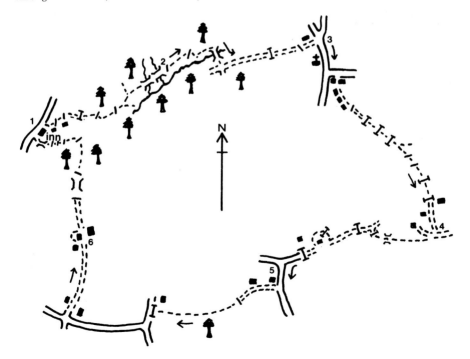

59

diagonally down the field to the gate at the far bottom corner. Go through, then over the stile ahead of you, cross the plank bridge, over another stile into the field and walk down the left-hand boundary to the stile in the hedge. Turn right through the gates and out onto the farm road.

4. Turn right at the junction and in twenty five yards take the footpath on the left. After about a quarter of a mile go over the footbridge, through the gate and straight ahead to the bridleway then turn left. Continue ahead through a small gate. The path is then diverted behind the barn and back down to the track. Leave by the gate and walk up the lane turning left at the road junction.

5. Walk up the hill turning right just past a house called Donny Brook. Go over the stile into the field and walk up to the stile at the top. Crossing the field the path follows a line to the right of the large oak then heads towards a gate on the left of the barn which takes you out into the road. Cross over, turn left and take the right-hand turn to Langhurst. At the crossroads turn right onto the farm track.

6. Follow the path between the farm buildings, out through the gate and immediately turn right following the field boundary behind the farmhouse and down to the bottom right-hand corner. Go over the stile into the woods, cross the plank bridge and stile and head up the field between the trees to the stile. Go over the brow of the hill, through a new tree plantation then over a stile, through the woods and over another stile. Half way along the hedgerow climb the stile into the wood, over one last stile, crossing the bridge out into the road and turn right back to the pub.

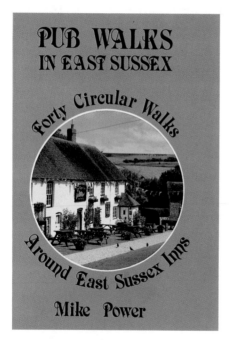

Available at £4.95

Available at £4.95

The raised path round Chidham peninsular, Walk No. 10

The bridge at Stedham, Walk No. 24

The Three Moles, Selham

When planning my books I try to include a variety of walks. I also look for a wide cross section of pubs. There are times after an enjoyable walk when all one wants is a cool drink in the friendly atmosphere of a typical village local. It is to these people that The Three Moles will appeal. This two storey pub, high up on the side of an embankment, was built in 1870 on the Pitts Hill Estate to serve the railway. Although the line has long since closed the pub still flourishes and is very much the village local. Two small cosy rooms, simply furnished, are served by the one bar. At the end is a games area and there are stuffed fish in cases on the wall. Each room has a fireplace with open fires in winter whilst outside there is a sheltered lawned beer garden with picnic benches - an ideal spot for warm summer days.

Today the pub is leased by King & Barnes, the Horsham Brewery. Their full range of real ales are available, all very well kept and dispensed by hand pump. There is Sussex Bitter, Broadwood - mid brown with a malty aroma, Festive and Mild Ale - smooth dark brown and malty, seasonal beers and Three Moles 'Second Best' Bitter specially brewed by King & Barnes to commemorate The Three Moles coming second in the CAMRA National Pub of the Year award.

The pub no longer serves food but has no objection to walkers bringing their own food for consumption OUTSIDE.

Children are not allowed inside the pub but there is no objection to well controlled dogs.

Monday to Friday opening hours are from 11.30 a.m. till 2.30 p.m. and again from 5.30 p.m. till 11 p.m. Saturday and Sunday all day.

Telephone: (01798) 861303.

Village just south from the A272 between Midhurst and Petworth

Approx. distance of walk: 4½ miles. OS Map No. 197 SU 935/206.

The inn has its own car park opposite but if you do not intend to visit the pub the licensee kindly requests that you do not use the car park - there is a lay-by by the phone box.

A most enjoyable walk across farm land, through woods and along bridleways.

1. From the inn turn right and take the first turning left. Continue past St James' church turning left when you reach the gravel track. Cross the old railway bridge and walk down to Smoky House. Ford through the stream and keep to the track ahead, through the gate into the field walking up to the little gate in the top hedge. Go through and follow the bridle path through the woods until you reach the junction of a footpath. Immediately go left over the stile and follow the path as it bears right, up through the woods then through a gate turning right into the road.

2. After passing houses on the right look for a signed footpath on the left. Follow this ill-defined path as it winds its way down into the woods eventually meeting with the bridleway at which point turn left. Ignore all side turnings and paths. After passing through pine woods the bridleway merges with the drive to a house leading to the lane.

3. Turn left, and after about a hundred yards take the signed footpath on the right into the woods. When you reach another bridleway turn left walking past bluebell woods turning right at the junction with the track. Simply follow the bridleway, past the farm buildings, out into the lane and turn left back to the inn, it is well signed.

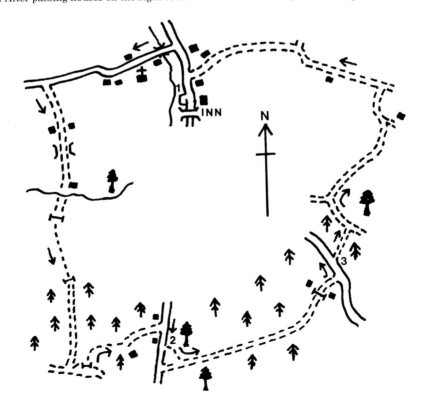

Crab & Lobster, Sidlesham

Sidlesham, on the western side of Pagham Harbour, was once a busy and prosperous port, it even had a wheat mill worked by the power of the tides. Now silted up it provides a natural haven for wildlife; over 180 different sorts of birds being seen each year. The Crab & Lobster is in a delightful position close to the quay. From the pretty back garden you look out across the meadows to the mud flats beyond. It has a long and interesting history, many tales having been told over the years but few of them considered to be true. Brian Cross, the landlord for the past 10 years, has never yet seen the supposed ghost. Two rooms lead off from the flag stoned hallway, both are comfortably furnished with open log fires, the plusher of the two having an interesting bar in the form of a boat.

The inn is a now a free house presently serving three real ales, Gales Butser Bitter, Arundel Stronghold and Skinner's Summer Haze.

The inn is included in many of the good pub guides for its excellent food and rightly so. Available seven days a week, except Sunday evening, you choose from the menu chalked on the blackboard. Snacks include toasted sandwiches, filled jacket potatoes and ploughman's, as well as tasty homemade soup, chicken liver and walnut pate, garlic prawns, escargot and smoked salmon. Selsey crab naturally features on the menu. Other dishes include fish pie, chilli, homemade steak & kidney pie, lasagne and a chicken curry. There are several traditional sweets like spotted dick, apple crumble and treacle tart.

Children are not allowed in either bar but there is no objection to dogs.

Weekday opening times are from 11 a.m. till 2.30.p.m.(3 p.m. Saturday) and from 6 p.m. till 11 p.m. Sunday 12 noon till 3 p.m. and 7 p.m. till 10.30 p.m.

Telephone: (01243) 641233.

Pub off the B2145 south from Chichester. Take either Rookery Lane or Mill Lane from the village centre.

Approx. distance of walk: 2¾ miles. OS Map No. 197 SZ 862/973.

The inn has its own car park but there is ample parking beside the old quay.

Sidlesham, once a busy port, is now a peaceful backwater; its silted harbour a haven for wildlife. The delightful walk takes you along the shore beside the Pagham Harbour Nature Reserve and back across farm land, it is easy going ideal for the whole family but waterproof footwear is advisable. Before planning the walk however first check the tide times, at high water the coastal path is flooded. It is only passable at low water.

1. From the pub you have two options either turn left directly onto the shore line and walk round keeping as close as possible to the bank on the left or turn right and walk up the lane until you reach a signed footpath leading down to the shore. Continue along the shore line ignoring the signed footpaths to the left and the right, but keep straight ahead on the raised path bordered with trees and scrub.

2. At the stile go into the field on the left and bear right across to the fence. Ignore the stile but continue beside the fence until you reach a second stile. Go into the field and bear left across to the finger post following the path ahead, through a small copse, then over the river and straight ahead across the field. Pass through the gap in the hedge opposite and follow the rough track, through a couple of gates and onto a farm road.

3. Further ahead there is a signed footpath on the left. Turn here following the well walked path across the field, to the left of a farm building and out into the lane. I was last here in May when the fields were a picture planted with bright yellow rape seed. Walk straight across into the field opposite turning left when you reach the boundary wall. The path then follows the edge of the field before bearing right back to the harbour.

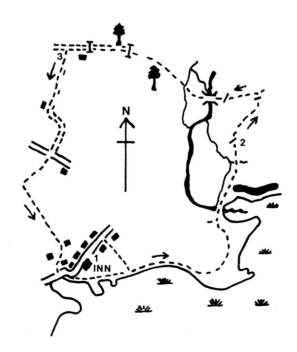

The Newburgh Arms, Slindon

Much of Slindon village is now the property of The National Trust but a few properties are still privately owned, one of them is The Newburgh Arms. Built sometime during the eighteenth century the name is derived from the family that once owned the Slindon estate. Colourful baskets adorn the exterior with more plants in tubs at the back. The attractive open plan bar has a beamed ceiling and is comfortably furnished and carpeted throughout with a warm winter log fire in one of two large fireplaces. One can eat in the main bar or in the dining area towards the back of the inn. Outside there is a sunny sheltered terrace behind the flint and brick wall.

The inn is a free house very well run by the owners, Dave and Julia Tanswell. Real ales include Badger Best from Hall & Woodhouse, the Dorset brewers and a selection from Gibbs Mew.

Good home cooked traditional bar food, plus an a la carte menu, is available seven days a week. There are dishes such as steak and kidney pie and rabbit pie, also a choice of salads, pork and bacon in cider and haddock in a prawn and mushroom sauce. Daily specials, chalked on the blackboard, might include bacon pudding, filled jacket potatoes, ploughman's, a curry, goulash, leg of lamb and a vegetarian chilli. In the restaurant there is a choice of fish, roasts or a cold carvery plus dishes such as jugged hare, pheasant casseroled in red wine, charcoal grilled steaks and beef stroganoff sauted with onions, mushrooms, sherry, brandy and cream.

Weekday opening times are from 11 a.m. till 2.30 p.m. and 6 p.m. till 11 p.m.

Families are welcome.

Overnight accommodation can be arranged.

Telephone: (01243) 814229.

Village signed off the A29 just north from the A27 at Fontwell.

Approx. distance of walk: 3 miles. OS Map No. 197 SU 965/084.

Park beside the pub or in the lane at the front.

A flat and easy walk through Slindon Woods mainly on large wide tracks. It is ideal for all members of the family.

1. From the inn turn right, walk up the hill and take the next turning right. At the bend continue straight ahead through the double gates onto the track. After a while you will see a finger post directing you left onto a footpath. Follow this path until it joins with a wide track and then turn left past Downe's Barn. Eventually you will reach the road by Slindon College. Continue ahead, ignoring the right-hand turn until you reach the turning on the left into Slindon Woods, you will see 'The National Trust' sign.

2. The entire property is owned by the National Trust and there are several different routes you can take. Unfortunately much of the mature beech wood was destroyed during the hurricane of 1989 and whilst many new trees have been planted it will be a generation before the woods are fully restored. The easiest route is to keep to the main track walking close to the field boundary on the left. The track eventually enters a small bluebell wood and afterwards joins with another track at which point turn right and walk towards the lane.

3. You can either go out into the lane and turn left then left into the field at the stile and across towards the red house leaving by the gate or keep to Slindon Wood and go through the gate on the left. The track follows the edge of the wood and emerges beside an attractive pond. Go out into the lane and turn right, past the village shop then left at the road junction up the hill back to the pub.

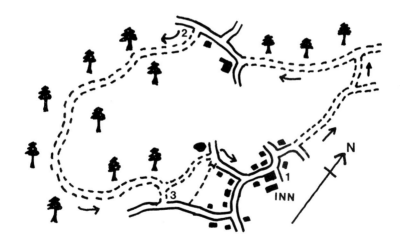

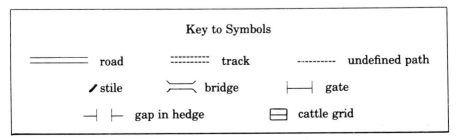

Key to Symbols

road   track   undefined path

stile   bridge   gate

gap in hedge   cattle grid

The Kings Head, Slinfold

Slinfold is a very pretty village with some attractive Georgian houses. The Kings Head itself was built in the early 15th century as an open hall house and became an ale house as far back as the 1600's. Many alterations and additions have been made over the years including the more modern exterior. The main bar has a carpeted floor, a beamed ceiling with copper and brass items and an open coal fire. There is an attractive a la carte dining room, a cosy back parlour with an open fire burning in an enormous inglenook fireplace and a separate comfortable family room with a flag stone floor. A terrace and award winning beer garden has views across open fields where there are lots of picnic benches, a barbecue and a childrens' area with rabbits.

It is a Whitbread house offering a good choice of their real ales which presently are Flowers Original, King & Barnes Sussex, Strong Country, Ballards and Boddington's Bitter.

A good food menu, much of it homemade, is served daily between 12 noon and 2 p.m. and from 7 p.m. till 10 p.m. Bar snacks include the usual ploughman's and sandwiches also homemade soup, shepherds pie, lasagne, chilli, vegetarian platter, fisherman's platter and Japanese prawns in a sweet and sour sauce with rice. The restaurant menu has ten starters which might include snails in garlic butter and deep fried Camembert, lots of steaks, Dover sole and rack of lamb. Weekday evening specials include blazing beans on Monday, curry on Wednesday, fish n'chips Friday, banger n'mash and spit roast on Sunday.

Weekday opening times are from 11 a.m. till 3 p.m. and 6 p.m. till 11 p.m. Sunday 12 noon till 10.30 p.m.

Children and dogs are equally welcome inside and out.

Accommodation available in four newly decorated rooms.

Telephone: (01403) 790339.

Slinfold is situated west of Horsham and can be reached either from the A29 or the A264.

Approx. distance of walk: 5 miles. OS Map No. 187 TQ 117/316.

Park at the pub or by the church.

A picturesque walk on farm land, through woods and across streams, ideal for the whole family.

1. Turn left from the pub walking past the church and into the minor road on the right towards the house. At the brow of the hill turn right onto the footpath walking away from the house and make your way down the field to the river at the bottom. Go right into the field and across keeping close to the hedge on the left. The track eventually crosses the river over a concrete bridge. Keep straight ahead bearing left over the hill following a line of oak trees between two fields. After the path dips into another river valley cross the wooden bridge into the woods beyond and follow the path up to the farm house. Walk round beside the boundary fence, out onto the drive and turn left along the farm road to reach the A29.

2. Cross over and follow the footpath ahead into the wood making your way uphill keeping as close as possible to the field boundary. As you approach the house on the brow look for a path sign and go right, over the stile and follow the fence round to the left then down the drive towards Rowhook turning left into the lane.

3. Just before reaching The Chequers, a handy half way watering hole, turn left and walk up to the junction. The footpath runs down the right-hand side of Burnt House. Walk up the drive and onto the footpath which follows the field and house boundary on the left leading into woodland. Continue along the bridleway and leave at the next signed footpath on the left. Walk down the hill bearing left at the path junction and further ahead, when you reach the crossing point of several paths, bear half right keeping to the public footpath then turn left onto the gravel track walking down to the main road and turn left.

4. Keep to the verge until you reach the bridleway on the opposite side then cross over and follow the track, over the bridge and past the house, through the farm stock yards and the gate on the far side. At the end of the concrete roadway go over the stile beside the gate on the left and walk down the field to the stile at the bottom. Cross the main road and turn right. At the signed footpath pass through the hedge into the field on the left and make your way across in the direction of the red bricked house, through two field boundaries and then bear left towards a couple more houses eventually out into a driveway, turning right back to the pub.

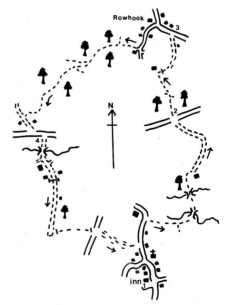

Key to Symbols		
══════ road	·········· track	---------- undefined path
✓ stile	⟩─⟨ bridge	├──┤ gate
─┤ ├─ gap in hedge	⊟ cattle grid	

The White Hart Inn, South Harting

The reputedly haunted White Hart Inn dates back to the 16th century and still today retains much of that original charm. Behind the two storey, white painted exterior are three traditional bars having beamed ceilings and inglenook fireplaces. Traditionally it is known as the home of the 'Old Club' the oldest known mens' club in England and in celebration every Whit Monday the pub is adorned with beech branches. Candles top the tables in the intimate restaurant, once the scullery, where on a cold winter's night diners can warm themselves by the enormous log fire burning in the hearth. There is a family room with childrens' toy box, picnic benches on the sunny front terrace and a beautiful garden.

The inn is a free house well run by the owners Angie and Allan Hayter. Real ales presently stocked are Tetley Bitter and Imperial, Burton Ale and Friary Meux Best Bitter.

Food is served all week except Monday evening from 12 noon till 2.30 p.m. and from 7 p.m. till 9.30 p.m. Apart from a choice of bar snacks such as sandwiches, ploughman's, salads, ham and chips and a steakwich, the restaurant menu includes moules bonne femme, Stilton and port country pate, smoked salmon mousse and mushrooms d'amour followed by lemon chicken - chicken fillets baked in a creamy lemon sauce and garnished with almonds, honey roast half duckling, boeuf bourguignon, chicken tikka masala, steak pepper pot, sizzling prawn Cantonese style, lamb and apricot bake, swordfish steaks and avocado and corn bake all served with a large selection of fresh seasonal vegetables and special saute potatoes.

Children have their own menu and ask to see the daily vegetarian selection. Weekday opening times are from 11 a.m. till 2.30 p.m. and 6 p.m. till 11 p.m.

Well behaved children are welcome and high chairs are available. There is no objection to dogs.

Telephone: (01730) 825355.

Village is on the B2146 about 3 miles from Petersfield.

Approx. distance of walk: 4 miles. OS Map No. 197 SU 784/194.

The pub has its own car park but there is also plenty of space in the village itself.

An enjoyable walk much of which is through woodland and in part on the South Downs Way and the Sussex Border Path.

1. Leave the pub and turn right and when you reach the car park take the short track on the right. Go through the gate and straight ahead across the park to pick up a track on the far side. It climbs gradually through woods to meet with the South Downs Way close to the road. Turn right and walk along the track for about a quarter of a mile until you reach a signed footpath on the left. Go up the bank, over the stile and turn right, through the hedge and over the stile on the left following the path into the trees.

2. In spring there are many bluebells and garlic smelling ransoms replaced in summer by spreading nettles and tall grass making walking a little difficult. Continue following the path up and over the stile, across the track, over a second stile and straight ahead. Ultimately you reach a stile giving access to a farm track. Turn right and follow it round to the left and then to the right into the woods forking right up to the bridleway and turn right. Eventually the track joins with a tarred drive which passes a farm and several dwellings before reaching the B2146.

3. Taking care cross over this busy road and go up onto the Sussex Border Path, it is signed. The path runs the whole way through the woods parallel with the lane on the left eventually dipping down to join it. Turn right, then right again at the road junction. Bear right at the next road junction and continue along the lane until you reach a signed footpath on the right and enter the field. Walk straight across to the far side, crossing the B2146 for a second time then walk up the track towards Church Farm. Before reaching the gates follow the little path on the left, round the buildings, out into the lane and turn left, past the church back to the village centre.

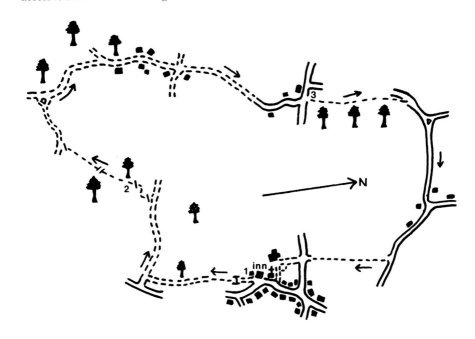

Hare & Hounds, Stoughton

Nestling beneath the South Downs in this peaceful and beautiful part of West Sussex is the Hare & Hounds. This handsome flint building, dating back to around the 17th century, was originally built as two cottages becoming a pub some eighty years ago. At that time one half was the village shop. Inside there are three rooms all inter-connected. The two at the front are comfortably furnished with a carpeted floor having part beamed ceilings and timber prop supports. Additional winter heating is provided by three open log fires. Two similar fireplaces are brick built in the style of a bee hive. The small, cosy rear public bar also has a fire, pew style bench seating, a close boarded timber floor with a dartboard and piano all adding to the village pub atmosphere. There are several picnic benches on the front terrace and a beer garden at the back.

The inn is a free house very well run by the owners Kathy and Peter Campbell. The well stocked bar includes a large and interesting wine list and an excellent choice of real ales which has warranted inclusion in The Good Beer Guide for the past 20 years. Typically there could be Fullers London Pride and Boddington's Bitter plus at least three or four guests such as the dark copper-red Old Baily from the Mansfield Brewery Company, Bishop's Tipple and Brakspear's Bitter.

Very good home cooked food is available seven days a week - all dishes freshly prepared on the premises. Each day there is usually a choice of delicious homemade soup also ploughman's jacket potatoes, home cooked gammon plus local crab and lobster salads, cheese and onion flan and chicken or mackerel pate. There is fresh fish and seasonal game, chicken Kiev and shepherds pie and the very popular steak and mushroom pie. The comprehensive sweet list includes Swedish chocolate and almond torte and rum pie.

Families are welcome and there is no objection to well behaved dogs.

Weekday opening times are from 11 a.m. till 3 p.m. and 6 p.m. till 11 p.m. Sunday 12 noon till 4 p.m. and 7 p.m. till 10.30 p.m.

Telephone: (01705) 631433.

From the A27 at Emsworth take the B2147 and then the B2146 turning right at the sign for Walderton. Stoughton is the next village along the road.

Approx. distance of walk: 4 miles. OS Map No. 197 SU 802/115

Park outside the inn at the front or near the village green.

Stoughton is an ancient village whose church alone dates back to the 11th century, but as with so many other villages probably suffered from the black death. This scenic walk takes you high up onto Bow Hill with its glorious viewpoint and ancient barrows with an optional walk through Kingley Vale; important for its yew forest. The going is fairly easy with no stiles or difficult sections but the walk up from the village is fairly steep.

1. From the pub turn right then left when you reach the signed bridleway beside Tythe Barn House. It is a long and gradual climb, steep in places, up a wide gravel track. At the top continue ahead ignoring the first signed bridleway into the forest but turn left when you reach the second, that is unless you wish to follow the path through the nature reserve. If you do continue ahead to the bottom corner of the field and follow the path into the forest. The reserve was established to maintain the yew forest which is the finest in Europe. The trail is way-marked and leaflets can be obtained from the nature reserve museum.

2. Both paths meet up close to the viewpoint on Bow Hill. A map on a stone pillar points out all the features to be seen. Continue ahead following the main track turning left at the junction of two bridleways. Continue down through the woods until the path joins with a wide gravel track. A few steps further ahead turn left at the cross track following the path between the wood on the right and the boundary fence of the field. The track widens as it gradually descends to meet the road at the bottom. Turn left back to the pub.

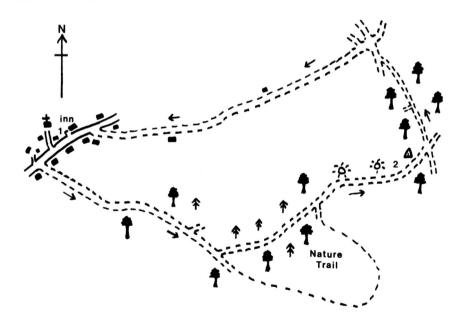

The Blue Ship, The Haven

The Victorian exterior belies the age of this remote and friendly unspoilt village pub. The main bar dates back to the fifteenth century. A well worn brick floor is evidence of the many customers who, over the centuries, have walked across to the small hatch where the ale is served. The low ceiling is heavily beamed and in the end wall is a large open fireplace with built in seats which has a warm log fire in winter. Simple furnishings consist of plain, scrubbed wooden tables and benches with high back wooden settles. Down the back corridor are two more rooms added in later years. There is also a separate games room with its own fireplace. Outside there are lots of seats in the cottage garden, and more on the terrace at the front.

It is a King & Barnes pub happily still serving real ale straight from the barrel. There are two, Sussex Bitter and the slightly stronger Broadwood, a mid-brown ale with a malty aroma.

Good homemade food is served at lunch time between noon and 2.15 p.m, and in the evening, except Sunday and Monday, from 7 p.m. till 9.15. p.m. Pub snacks include sausages with bread, ploughman's and sandwiches. Also chalked on the blackboard are dishes such as ratatouille au gratin, cheesy cottage pie, lasagne, steak and kidney pie, salads, scampi, cod and chips, tuna bake and ham with two eggs and chips. For 'afters' there is fruit crumble, treacle tart and grannies wedding cake which, I am told, is homemade bread pudding.

Children are only allowed in the back rooms but there is no objection to dogs.

Opening times are from 11 a.m. till 3 p.m. and 6 p.m. till 11 p.m. Sunday 12 noon till 4 p.m. and 7 p.m. till 10.30 p.m.

Telephone: (01403) 822709.

Turn off the A29 after Five Oaks and take the turning to Haven then follow the signpost left towards Garlands and Okehurst.

Approx. distance of walk: 8 miles. OS Map No. 187 TQ 084/305

There is good parking at the pub also a lay-by in the road opposite.

An enjoyable walk along country lanes, on bridleways and footpaths, through woods and along The Wey South Path beside the old canal. Waterproof footwear is recommended as some of the paths do become very muddy in wet weather.

1. Turn right from the pub, walk down the road and bear left at the junction towards Gibbons Mill turning right when you reach the farm road. Keep straight ahead at the farm house following the bridleway to the bottom of the hill and cross the concrete bridge into the field ahead. On the far side cross a second bridge and make your way up the track until you eventually come to a stile in the hedge on the left beyond a brick entrance to a large house, it is signed. Follow the path, which can become overgrown in summer, up to another stile and bear left across the field to the gate in the corner. Walk past the house, over the stile in the hedge and turn right along the drive turning left into the road.
2. At the bottom of the hill go through the gate on the right, across the field turning half right onto The Wey South Path. It is a

pleasant walk following the old canal which is presently being lovingly restored by volunteers. Cross the farm road at Barnshill Bridge and continue along the tow path, through a gate and eventually out into the lane turning left.
3. Half way up the hill turn left onto the concrete road walking until you reach the signed footpath on the left. Follow it round to the gate and go through into the woods beyond. Keep to the main track ahead and after about 150 paces take the footpath on the right. In 50 yards cross the plank bridge and carry on through the woods turning right onto the signed footpath at the top of the hill. When you reach the gravel track turn left, and in a couple of hundred yards take the signed bridleway on the right. Keep straight ahead between two fields turning right into the lane.

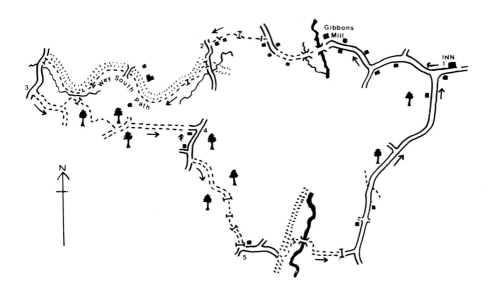

4. After crossing the bridge turn left onto the bridleway. Ignore the side tracks but keep straight ahead through the farm gate and fork left. Follow the track through a gate into the field keeping straight ahead to the gate opposite and across the field following the hedge to the gate in the right-hand corner. The track beyond takes you up past farm buildings and out through a gate onto the track.

5. Turn left, pass through a couple of gates then bear left over the canal turning left onto the bridleway. Go through the gate onto the track making a right turn at the bridge, enter the field and walk across bearing half right, out onto the track then through the gate, up to the lane and turn left back to the pub.

The Wey South Path beside the old canal

Volunteers restoring the old canal

The Horseguards Inn, Tillington

Upon entering the ancient village of Tillington one is immediately struck by the distinctive coronet on All Hallows church tower. Opposite, high above the road, is the charming Horseguards Inn said to have been named after the regiment billeted in Petworth Park during the Napoleonic Wars. Built originally as three cottages they were knocked through over the years creating the now charming pub. The one main bar is heated in winter by an open fire. From the large box window seat there is a lovely view to the Rother Valley. Three other rooms, all on different levels, simply burst with character. One has just a rug on the bare brick floor, plain walls, simple furnishings and a warm open log fire. Another has an assortment of old tables, chairs and settles whilst the third cosy room has timber and plastered walls, a small stove and country style pine furniture. A small terrace at the front has a couple of tables with more on the lawn at the back.

The inn is a free house very well run by the owners. A very good wine list is available plus two real ales, Badger Best and King & Barnes Sussex.

The inn is restaurant orientated specialising in fresh fish. All meals are cooked on the premises even the bread rolls. The limited snack menu includes plough-man's and sandwiches and usually tasty homemade soup. At lunch time there are dishes such as skate wing cooked in black butter with capers, grilled whole plaice and two roasts. The evening menu might include courgette and cheese mousse, avocado with seafood in garlic mayonnaise, and chicken liver parfait followed by fillet of turbot garnished with prawns in a lime and butter sauce, rack of English lamb on a bed of ratatouille with a rosemary sauce or half a roast guinea fowl.

Weekday opening times are from 11 a.m. till 3 p.m. and 6 p.m. till 11 p.m. Sunday 12 noon till 3 p.m. and 7 p.m. till 10.30 p.m.

Children are welcome and dogs allowed in some areas.

Accommodation is available in three double en suite rooms.

Telephone: (01798) 342332.

Walk No. 33

Village is just off the A272 between Midhurst and Petworth.

Approx. distance of walk: 5 miles. OS Map No. 197 TQ 963/220

There is a small car park at the rear of the inn but it is better to park in the lane at the front.

A very enjoyable walk, through woods, across farm land and along country lanes. It also passes beside a tributary of the Rother and through the hamlets of Upperton and River. Although easy for most of the way some sections can be very tricky especially when wet.

1. Leave the inn and turn left walking up the lane beside the wall of Petworth House. Continue through Upperton and beyond the turning to Pitshill. Ignore the first signed footpath on the left but keep going until you reach a second, almost opposite the monument. There are two paths take the right fork which steers you fairly steeply down into a bluebell wood.

2. Follow the path and after leaving the wood turn left onto the track then bear right along another track passing the dwelling on the right. Continue ahead until you reach a finger post on the left, go over the stile into the field and bear left. Pass through the gap in the opposite hedge and continue across making for the left-hand side of the farm buildings. Walk past the finger post bearing right down to the gate, cross the bridge and turn left. Keep to the track until it bears left down a short grass track to a gate. Go through, over the stream and turn left walking round the field keeping fairly close to the boundary and the river on the left. Eventually when you reach the stile continue straight ahead then walk round be-

hind the back of a farm house, over a stile and down to the lane.

3. Walk straight across and climb the stile into the field bearing right to the stile set in the far hedge. Follow the path through the trees to the stile on the far side then walk across the field, over another stile and back into woodland. Keeping close to the stream, continue ahead over the stile into the field ahead, across to a pair of stiles and over to one last stile.

4. Go over and turn left making for the finger post. Pass through the gate, cross the bridge and take the path on the left this time with the river on your left. The path meanders through woods rising to a clearing to meet a wider forest track. Turn left and further on fork left up to the stile following the path between the dwellings, over the stile into the lane at River and turn left.

5. After just a short distance take the signed footpath on the right. Go over the stile, up the path and climb the steps through a small bluebell wood. Negotiate the stile at the top, walk across the gully, up more steps and

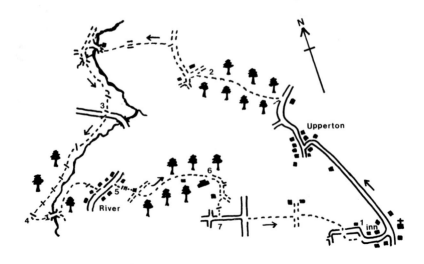

bear left following the narrow path round the bank. Care is necessary at times as the path becomes overgrown in summer and can be slippery; to make matters worse in places the path slopes away from the hill and there are a number of fallen trees.

6. The path eventually rises to meet a wider track close to the tower and then gradually descends onto the lawns of the house at Pitshill. Continue straight ahead keeping to the main drive, over the stile beside the cattle grid and continue down ignoring the path on the left. As you round the bend there is a row of oaks, turn right across the grass and head towards the dwelling. On the left you will see a stile leading into a thicket, go over walking down through the trees to meet the lane and turn left.

7. The rhododendron hedge on the left can be a picture in the spring. At the road junction walk straight across onto the path between the fields, then through the gate, across the gully, over the tarred track and into the field. Make you way towards the village, go out into the lane and turn left. Alternately you can continue straight ahead through the cemetery it will bring you out to meet the lane on the far side.

The Tower close to Pitshill House

The Keepers Arms, Trotton

Set on a rise above the road this popular village pub is highly spoken of by the locals. Originally a blacksmith's shop and private dwelling the owners at the time started selling ale and named it the Blue Anchor. Chichester Brewery eventually acquired the pub. It was not until 1972 that it was purchased as a free house. The attractive main bar has a beamed ceiling with cottage style furniture and is warmly carpeted throughout. It angles round into a similar dining area. The pub is perfectly placed with a south facing front terrace which gets the sun all day – especially the sunset.

A free house the inn is very well run by the present owners Jenny and Steve Oxley who took over in 1996. The well stocked bar offers a very interesting and extensive wine list including some interesting Chateau bin ends and three real ales, Marston's Pedigree, Old Speckled Hen and Wadworth 6X.

The Keepers Arms is a popular place to eat offering an extensive menu six days a week available from 12 noon till 2.30 p.m. and 7 p.m. till 9.30 p.m. The choice ranges from French onion soup to half a kilo of moules mariniere and an eight bone rack of lamb in a rich redcurrant and rosemary sauce cooked on the chargrill. There are some excellent vegetarian meals such as pancakes and pasta dishes plus daily specials. Fondues are the house speciality; try warming yourself with a Swiss cheese fondue or alternatively a Chinois fondue of thin fillet of beef cooked in a stock at the table.

Children, dogs and ramblers are all equally welcome.

Weekday opening times are from 11 a.m. till 2.30 p.m. and from 6 p.m. till 11 p.m. The pub is closed all day Monday except for bank holidays.

Telephone: (01730) 813724.

The village of Trotton lies on the A272 east of Petersfield.

Approx. distance of walk: 3½ miles. OS Map No. 197 SU 838/223.

The inn has its own fairly large car park.

A very enjoyable walk mostly flat and easy going which takes you first along the banks of the River Rother passing through the hamlets of Iping and the delightful village of Stedham. The second half of the walk is across Stedham, Iping and Trotton Common Nature Reserves.

1. From the inn make your way left along the A272. Just before the bridge you will see a signed footpath on the right. Go over the stile and straight ahead through a marshy area towards a stile in the right-hand fence. Cross into the adjoining field making your way over to the stile in the corner then follow the path down to the lane and turn left.

2. On the right, opposite a row of three cottages, look for a signed footpath and follow it beside the ditch and up the bank. Further ahead a stile takes you onto the path beside the wood and into a field. After passing through a small bluebell wood and crossing a bridge a dog leg in the path steers you through a gate into a large field, it is all well signed.

3. On the far side pass through the gate, head straight across the lane at Iping and up the signed bridleway opposite. Walk past the coach house and go through the metal gate on the right. It is a very pretty path especially in the spring when part of the

river bank is carpeted in a colourful display of bluebells and lilac coloured cuckoo flowers. When you reach Stedham turn right walking through this delightful village up to the main road.

4. Go straight across on the Minsted road turning right at the signed bridleway onto Stedham Common. Keep to the main track then cross the road and bear left through the car park onto Iping Common Nature Reserve. Tracks cross in all directions but keep to the main path turning left when you reach a signed bridleway.

5. Upon Entering the woods almost immediately turn right onto the bridleway and follow the path across a track and onto a narrow path up the heath to meet a track at the top then turn right. It is very wide in places with many signed paths leading off but ignore all these until you reach a bridleway signed down a sandy track on the left. At the bottom simply turn right back to the pub.

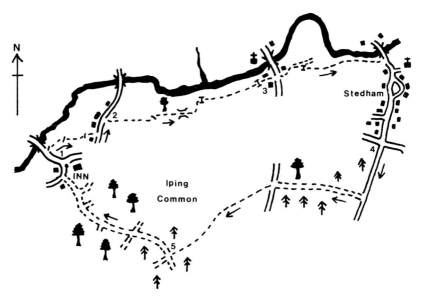

81

The Barley Mow, Walderton

Entering the picturesque village of Walderton one's attention is immediately drawn to the attractive exterior of The Barley Mow. Apart from the many tubs of plants, window boxes and hanging baskets one end wall is completely draped in a mantle of flowering clematis. Inside are several inter-connected rooms. The front part of the bar still has the original flag stone floor with a small raised wood burning fire in the centre wall. There is another log fire in one of the seating areas. Comfortable furniture consists of arm chairs and padded wall settles. Two further rooms at the back, right and left of the bar, are similarly furnished. On the walls are many old interesting photographs and garage receipts. There are picnic benches at the front and many more attractive wooden tables and chairs in the family garden at the side and running down to the stream in the back garden. The inn also has its own skittle alley.

It is a free house well run by the owners Colin and Lynne Ive. The well stocked bar offers a good selection of wines plus five real ales: Ringwood's Old Thumper, Wadworth 6X, Courage Best, Ruddles and John Smiths.

Good home cooked food, available seven days a week from 11 a.m. till 2.30 p.m. and 6 p.m. till 10 p.m. includes snacks such as homemade soups, ploughman's, jacket potatoes and freshly cut sandwiches. Main course meals might include local venison steaks home cooked in the pub's own game sauce, homemade steak and mushroom pie and vegetarian dishes like vegetable curry.

Families are welcome and there is no objection to dogs.

The inn is open during the week from 11 a.m. till 2.30 p.m. and from 6 p.m. till 11 p.m.

Telephone: (01705) 631321.

The village is best reached from the A27 at Emsworth. Take the B2147 and then the B2146. The village is signed.

Approx. distance of walk: 6¼ miles. OS Map No. 197 SU 790/106

The pub has its own large car park but you can also park safely in Cooks Lane or by the green.

A very enjoyable walk across fields, through woods and along bridleways, passing close to Stansted House and Racton Monument. Although a fairly long walk it is easy going for most of the way except for the steep climb up through Watergate Hanger.

1. Leave the pub and turn left then left again into Cooks Lane. Continue up and round until you reach a signed footpath on the right. Walk round behind the house, go over the stile into the field and straight across following the line of the power cables. Cross the track and maintain direction heading for the stile in the corner by the L shaped strip of woodland. Bear right down the field to the stile in the far fence, cross the track and go over the stile into the lane turning right.

2. Walk up and round and, upon reaching a building on the right with a colonnade front, take the small path up the bank opposite to meet the bridleway and turn right. At the crossing point of another bridleway turn left onto the track which climbs steeply up through the woods. In spring it is dotted with numerous violets and carpeted in places with garlic smelling ramsons.

3. At the top bear left and continue ahead along the gravel track until it merges with a tarred drive. Walk past Lumley Seat and further on go through the gate turning right. After passing the entrance to Stansted House turn left into the field and follow the bridleway along the boundary, out onto the track at the far side and turn right. Walk through the car park and bear left, across the field to the hedge proceeding until you reach a stile. Cross into the field and bear right over to the stile in the far hedge, go out onto the bridleway and turn left. The track is fairly long passing beside Racton Monument before descending to meet the road.

4. Turn left keeping to the grass verge then cross the stile into the field on the left and bear right across to the gate after which make for the kissing gate in the corner by the building. Turn left, cross the bridge and then turn right onto the lawn in front of the large house following the course of the stream across to the small gate on the far side. Proceed to the stile and continue straight ahead to one stile in the far fence. Cross the field turning right into the lane and bear left up to the main road. Walk straight across into Cooks Lane following it back to the pub.

The Frankland Arms, Washington

The Frankland Arms, built around 1795, was originally known as The Washington Inn. The pub was owned by Henry Michell a brewer from Horsham but he was eventually taken over by The Rock Brewery in 1911 which subsequently went to Whitbread. The inn was re-named in honour of William Frankland of Muntham Court. The attractive exterior is adorned with many flower troughs and hanging baskets. Inside the lounge bar is comfortably furnished with part wood panelled walls and heated by a warm log fire in the large inglenook fireplace. Interestingly the area behind the fireplace is lit in winter by natural gas lighting. A separate, attractive country style public bar has a beamed ceiling also with a fire in winter. Walkers are welcome but the landlord would prefer us to use the garden entrance where a room is provided for keeping back packs. There is a separate restaurant area and an attractive beer garden where barbecues are held in summer.

Three or four real ales are regularly available in this well managed house which include Flowers Original, London Pride, Boddington's Best Bitter and Boddington's Mild.

Food is available seven days a week between 12 noon and 2.30 p.m. and 6.30 p.m. till 9.30 p.m. The lunchtime menu is mostly snacks such as ploughman's, sandwiches and toasties with a larger menu available in the evening. Blackboards list the daily specials which usually include four dishes plus two homemade pies, fresh fish and steaks.

Children are allowed in the public bar, dogs in garden only.

Weekday opening times are from 11 a.m. till 11 p.m. Sunday 12 noon till 10. 30 p.m.

Telephone: (01903) 892220.

The pub is just off the A283 east from its junction with the A24 about 7 miles north from Worthing.

Approx. distance of walk: 6¼ miles. OS Map No. 198 TQ 124/127.

The pub has a large car park but you can also park in the wide road at the front or in the lane at the side.

A ridge walk with beautiful views. At first a moderate climb to the ridge then easy walking.

1. Leave the pub and turn right. Almost opposite Stocks Mead there is a stile in the fence, go over and bear right, over a second stile and across the field towards a stile leading into the woods. Make your way up the steep path, past the quarry where you join with the South Downs Way then turn left. Keep walking along the gravel track until the path levels and joins with another track then turn left.

2. Further ahead there is stile on the left which leads into an inclosure with a dew pond. Restored in 1970 by the Society of Sussex Downsmen, the pond was first constructed in 1870. Dew ponds tend to occur only on the chalk downs and in there day were sometimes the only source of water for the sheep. They rarely failed even in the severest draught. Bear right over the stile and walk to the triangulation point where you have a glorious view of the surrounding countryside. Return to the track and turn left, past Chanctonbury Rings, through a gate beside the cattle grid and continue walking for little over a mile until you see a footpath marker sign on the left.

3. Turn off the South Downs Way and follow this path along the field boundary turning right at the far left-hand corner. Fork left at the finger post down through the woods following the main path. Just before reaching the road cross the stile into the field on the left and, keeping close to the field boundary on the right, walk across, through into a second field maintaining direction until a finger post directs you up into a wood. Cross the stream and work your way up to the stile then bear half right over to another stile to meet the track.

4. When you reach the lane turn left and continue ahead under the footbridge. At the top of the lane pass round the gate turning right when you reach an off set cross junction, just past the farm buildings, then go immediately left keeping straight ahead through a metal gate into the woods. Walk up and over the hill then down through the trees to a gate. Leave the woods turning half right, cross the field making for the gap in the hedge, the path is signed. Walk diagonally across the next field to a short fence, turn along it and walk down the track, past the farm buildings turning right twenty yards further upon reaching the signed footpath.

5. Go over the stile and diagonally left across the field making for the stile in the far corner. Turn left walking to the right of the cattle trough then over the stile in the fence by the white house. Cross the concrete farm road, over a second stile between two fences climbing one last stile at the bottom. Cross the plank bridge, go through the gate and diagonally across the field leaving by the kissing gate back to the pub.

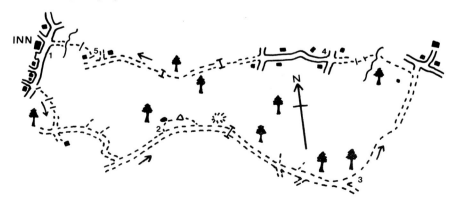

The Royal Oak, Wineham

Throughout the county of Sussex there are, happily, still many old delightful country pubs, typical village locals maintaining the traditions of centuries. The lovely Royal Oak, set back from the road with open fields beyond, is one of my favourites. The building dates back to the fourteenth century and has been a pub for some 200 years. From the simple black and white timbered exterior entering through the half stable door is to step back in time. Hung from the attractive low beamed ceilings of the main bar, and snug beyond, and around the walls are numerous old artifacts. The floor is part flag and part boarded worn with age, the furniture simple and old fashioned. In winter there is a warm log fire in an enormous inglenook fireplace. One interesting feature I have not seen in any other pub is an open fireplace actually behind the bar; very pleasant I would imagine for the bar staff in winter. Outside there are lots of picnic benches on the lawns surrounding the pub.

The inn is a Whitbread tenancy where real ale is still served traditionally straight from the barrel. Presently there is a choice of three, Wadworth 6X, Pompey Royal and Harveys Best from the East Sussex brewery.

The pub is first and foremost an ale house not a restaurant the only food available are ploughman's, sandwiches, plain or toasted and warming winter soups.

Opening times during the week are from 11 a.m. till 2.30 p.m. and 5.30 p.m. (Saturday 6 p.m.) till 11 p.m. Sunday 12 noon till 3 p.m. and 7 p.m. till 10.30 p.m.

Children are not allowed inside the main bar but there is a separate family room outside. There is no objection to dogs.

Telephone: (01444) 881252.

Village signposted south from the A272 and north from the B2116.

Approx. distance of walk: 5½ miles. OS Map No. 198 TQ 236/206.

There is a small parking area directly in front of the pub and a larger car park to the side.

A fairly level enjoyable walk across farm land, on bridleways, through woods which takes you along the River Adur.

1. Leave the Royal Oak turning right, walk for about 200 yards then turn left onto the farm track at a house named Gatefield. Continue past the farm house turning left at the cross track, then right when you reach a metalled road and head towards the farm buildings. Look for the foot path on the right-hand side, just past a large oak, and go into the field following the line of the hedgerow to the bottom left-hand corner. Cross the little stream and continue ahead keeping to the hedge on the left. Go over the stile and bear diagonally to the bridge. On the far side, keeping close to the hedge on the left, take the right-hand footpath towards the pylons then turn left through the second gateway, it is marked. The path follows close to the hedge on the left up and over the brow of the hill. Go through the kissing gate and make your way across to the far left-hand corner of the field where there is a stile beside the gate. Cross over if you wish to visit the 16th century church of St. Peter.

2. From the stile continue along the left-hand fence line towards the farm. Pass through the gate into the yard and keep straight ahead onto the concrete farm road, through a second gate and down the hill. Cross the River Adur then immediately turn right along the river bank. Go through a gap in the hedge and look for a path sign on your left taking you through the left-hand hedge. Enter into the field and turn right along the hedgerow. Cross over the stile in the bottom right-hand corner and, keeping close to the hedge on the right, walk across the field, over the stile and continue ahead. Turn left at the bottom of the field walking until you reach a gate on the right, go through and up a grass track between trees. Pass through the farmyard, out through the gate, cross the main road and turn left.

3. Take the second turning on the right and sharp right up the grass track, past Roma Farm to the brow of the hill to meet a metalled road leading to Abbeylands Farm.

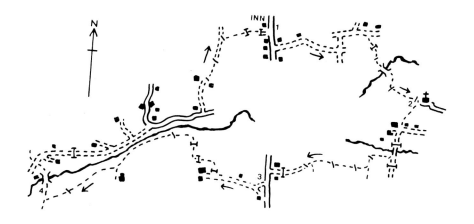

The sketch maps in this book are not necessarily to scale but have been drawn to show the maximum amount of detail.

Walk No. 37

Just before the farm go through the gate on the right and bear left between an open barn and stock pens, through a second gate and immediately turn right. Leave by the gate at the bottom of the field and turn left following the river, cross the stile beside the weir and continue ahead until you eventually reach a stile by the brick weir station.

4. Go up the incline and over the bridge to pick up the footpath behind the brick building leading up to a bridleway. Turn right and make your way back along the track. Pass through the gate and continue ahead ignoring the side turnings until you reach the lane beyond the cattle grid then turn right. Turn left, when you reach the driveway to 'Springlands' enter the field gate on the west side of the drive, 100 yards south of the house, keep to the west side of the barn and pond then east of the wood and cross the stile into the field turning left. Keeping close to the fence, walk round to the stile in the corner and go out onto the track. Continue ahead and then bear right over the stile onto the signed footpath. Follow the fence on the right, through a couple of gates then over the stile walking beside the hedge on the left, turning right though the gate to the pub.

St. Laurence's, Lugashall, Walk No. 21

All Saints, East Dean, Walk No. 12

St. Mary The Virgin, Burpham, Walk No. 6

The Richmond Arms, West Ashling

West Ashling is one of several pretty hamlets in this delightful county. The houses and cottages are clustered close to the old mill with its attractive mill pond. The friendly village local has two comfortably furnished bar areas both with open fires and one with a bar billiard table. Above the part wood panelled walls you will notice several numbered wooden ducks which are used at times for duck racing in the nearby river. A cosy skittle alley also has an open fire. Outside at the front is a small terrace with picnic benches under a pergola.

The inn is a free house well run by the owners Bob & Chris Garbutt. It is positively a real ale drinkers delight; at any one time there can be as many as ten to choose from. Three regular beers include Boddington's Bitter, King & Barnes Festive, Marstons Pedigree, Harveys Mild and Fremlins Bitter but some one hundred different guest beers are dispensed over a twelve month period. Beers such as Timothy Taylor Landlord, Robinswood Old Fart, Uley's Pigor Mortis and Crouch Vale Willie Warmer to name but a few.

Good home cooked food is always available and listed on the blackboard in the bar. There are snacks such as homemade soup, jacket potatoes, sandwiches and ploughman's. Main meals include Barnsley lamb chops, cottage pie, lasagne and gammon with eggs. Besides farmhouse mixed grill other popular dishes include croque monsieur - three pieces of bread one with ham, one with cheese, coated in egg and grilled. Texas brunch is garlic bread, a six ounce steak with two fried eggs.

The inn is open during the week from 11 a.m. till 3 p.m. and again from 5.30 p.m. till 11 p.m. Sunday 12 noon till 10.30 p.m.

Families are welcome, dogs too.

Telephone: (01243) 575730.

The inn is best reached from the A27 then the B2146. Turn left into Southbrook Road then right at the T junction.

Approx. distance of walk: 4½ miles. OS Map No. 197 SU 805/074.

As parking is rather limited at the pub you may have to find a spot close by. It is just possible to park in the lane at the front.

A most enjoyable walk, fairly flat and easy going although often muddy in places during wet weather. It take you across farm land, through the small villages of Funtington and East Ashling and through a couple of bluebell woods.

1. Leave the inn and turn left, turning right when you reach School Dell. Continue along the gravel track past the playing field and go over the stile into the field on the right. Bearing slightly left walk across to meet a grass track then follow it straight ahead, round the far end of the field and over the stile into the churchyard. Go out through the front gate, turn left, walk up to the main road and turn right.

2. Keep walking through the village until the road bears right then cross over into Downs Lane. After passing the entrance to Downs Farm turn right upon reaching the signed bridleway. Further ahead cross the lane and continue ahead into the woods, another area sadly decimated in the great storm of 89. Keep going turning right when you reach the signed footpath, following it straight ahead, up to the lane and turn right.

3. Turn left at the road junction walking past The Horse & Groom crossing over when you reach the bend then go through the kissing gate onto the signed footpath. Cross the stile into the field, turn left and then go through the gate into the adjoining field. Turn right, walk to the bottom then turn right through the farm gate and follow the fence to the corner. Go over the stile into the field ahead and turn left walking to the bottom, over the stile back into the field then cross the stile into the wood.

4. Keep to the main path which although attractive can be very muddy when wet. When you eventually reach the stile go into the field, straight ahead through a couple of gates then over the stile beside the house turning right into the lane. After joining with the A27 continue ahead. Although not a very busy road it is best to proceed with care. After a short distance turn left into Southbrook Road, cross the river and go over the stile into the field on the right. The path will take you straight back to the pub.

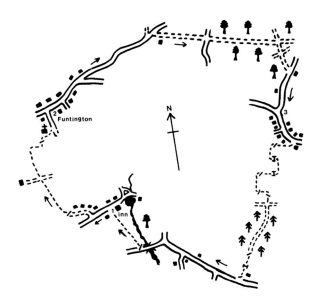

The Cat Inn, West Hoathly

West Hoathly is an ancient village first mentioned in 765. The parish church was built by the Normans in 1096. Nearby Gravetye Manor House, now a smart country hotel, was until 1935 the home of William Robinson. He was described as perhaps the greatest gardener of his time and whilst at Gravetye planted one of the finest collections of trees in the country. The estate is now administered by the Foresty Commission. The friendly and peaceful 300 year old pub, with its tile hung front above white brickwork, is adorned in summer with lots of hanging baskets and tubs giving a colourful touch. There is seating on a sunny narrow front terrace overlooking the church opposite. Inside the open plan bar has a high beamed ceiling, part panelled walls and a massive inglenook fireplace. A passage-way at the side leads through to a similar sized room, comfortably furnished with padded wooden settles. There is a separate restaurant at the back.

The inn is a Beards pub (who no longer brew). There are usually two real ales; at present Adnams Bitter and Harveys Bitter with Old Ale in winter.

Bar snacks, chalked on the blackboard and available all week with a limited Sunday lunch time menu but no food on Sunday evenings, include sandwiches, decent ploughman's, rolls, homemade soup and smoked salmon and crab pate with main dishes such as lasagne, curry, chicken liver with mushrooms, pork in Madeira and various steaks. Fish features very strongly on the menu with seasonal dishes such as fresh whole lobster and crab, also fresh salmon in puff pastry, fresh grilled sardines, halibut, red mullet and seafood thermido. A separate restaurant menu has additional dishes such as poisson Madeira, quails au poivre, and half a duck.

Children are not allowed in the bar and only in the restaurant if accompanying their parents for a meal. Dogs are not allowed at all.

Weekday opening times are from 11 a.m. till 2.30 p.m. and 6 p.m. till 11 p.m. Telephone (01342) 810369.

From Crawley take the A264 and then the B2028 south taking the turn for West Hoathly. Alternatively coming from Ardingly turn right into Cobb Lane, up and over Horncombe. The pub is on the road junction opposite the church.

Approx. distance of walk: 5½ miles OS Map No. 187 TQ 362/325.

The pub has its own car park but you can also safely park in the road by the church.

A very nice family walk mostly on well defined country tracks taking you through woods, across farm land and through the grounds of Gravetye Manor Estate.

1. Leave the pub turning right, cross the road and go over the stile in the fence on the right-hand side of the bus shelter. Walk past the houses, through the gap in the hedge and onto the track. Go over the stile into the field and straight ahead to a second stile beside the gate. Follow the track through a gateway after which it joins with a farm road.

2. Eventually when you reach the junction turn half right keeping to the signed path down the hill and in twenty yards go through the kissing gate into woods on the right, through a second kissing gate and over the stile into an open field. Keep straight ahead up to the stile beside the gate, turning right into the field beyond, over a small stile then straight ahead to a stile beside the gate.

3. When the path emerges onto a track turn left, walk up to the road, cross over turning left again. Turn right just before Duckyls

Farm then go over the stile and bear half right down the hillside to the stile in the fence at the bottom. Cross into the field and bear diagonally left to a stile in the corner. In the field beyond continue in the same direction to a plank bridge in the corner, cross over and turn left onto a metalled estate road walking uphill past Gravetye Manor. The grounds are open to the public, Tuesdays and Fridays only, from 10 a.m. till 5.p.m.

4. Turn left at the junction then right on the track towards Home Farm. Walk past the farm, through the trees and take the right fork at the next path junction. In twenty yards fork left and keep straight ahead down through the woods and over a small bridge, the path is well marked. After bearing left and passing under the high voltage electricity cables take the path on the right, turning right into the lane.

5. Bear left at the junction and left again

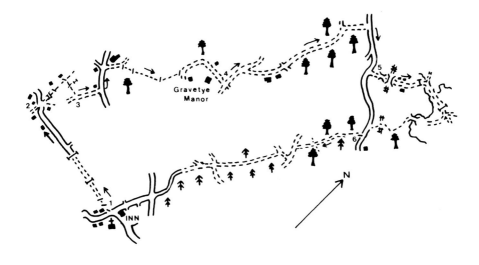

The sketch maps in this book are not necessarily to scale but have been drawn to show the maximum amount of detail.

Walk No. 39

upon reaching the bridleway, cross the bridge walking up the hill under the disused railway arch. After passing the farm buildings go through the gate, over the river and turn immediately right following the track through the field up to the gate and take the right-hand track. Take the signed path on the right upon reaching the brow of the hill. Bearing half right cross the stream and turn left under the power lines, up the field into woodland. Go up and over the old railway embankment taking the path ahead, turning left into the lane.

6. In twenty five yards cross the stile into the field on the right and walk up into the woods. Follow the path ahead until you reach the main track then turn left. After fifty yards take the right-hand turn and then immediately follow the footpath on the left. Keep straight ahead at the cross tracks and bear left at the fork up to a larger track. It merges with a metalled road ahead and eventually meets the B2028. Cross over into North Lane keeping straight ahead back to the pub.

Walk No. 21

Walk No. 26

The Lamb Inn, West Wittering

This charming roadside inn was originally constructed as a private house and dates back to the 18th century. Apparently it became licensed following an incident when the occupant, Mr Bard, accompanied by friends, purchased a barrel of beer from the Bell Inn at Birdham. He took it home and afterwards successfully applied for a licence. Today it is a free house very well run and beautifully kept by the owners, Nigel & Jo Carter who took over the licence in 1989. The main L shaped bar has a timber propped beamed ceiling, parquet wood flooring and comfortable polished wooden settles. At either end are open fireplaces, one having a warm log fire. There is a similarly furnished middle bar and beyond that a small but very comfortable dining area. Outside there is plenty of seating on the attractive front terrace and more in the beer garden at the rear.

Three very well kept real ales are served by hand pump they are Bunce's Best, Ballards Bitter and Ringwood's '49er' plus at least one guest beer.

The Lamb is no exception today in offering a very good food menu but it is nice to see when the emphasis is pub first and restaurant second. The lunchtime bar menu, served between 12 noon and 2 p.m, is chalked on the blackboard above the fireplace. Toasted sandwiches are the speciality. Other snacks include homemade soup and ploughman's, also their own homemade pies. A larger evening menu, served between 7 p.m. and 9 p.m, except Sunday evening, offers a good choice of steaks, beef lasagne and fresh fish such as brill and usually a vegetarian dish like spinach and mushroom bake. Delicious puddings include treacle tart, glu glu sponge and apricot tart.

Children are allowed in the pub but only when accompanied and kept under control.

Weekday opening times are from 11 a.m. till 2.30 p.m. and 6 p.m. till 11 p.m.

Telephone: (01243) 511105.

Walk No. 40

Pub on the B2179 between Birdham and West Wittering.

Approx. distance of walk: 4¾ miles. OS Map No.197 SZ 804/993.

Apart from the inn's own car park it is possible to park on the verge at the front.

An interesting level walk through Shipton Green down to West Itchenor returning along the shore and across fields.

1. Leave the inn and turn right. After passing the entrance to a house go over the stile on the right and follow the footpath beside the ditch, over a couple of stiles and out into the lane. Turn right and continue ahead at the road junction through Shipton Green to West Itchenor. There are many delightful and some unusual properties all the way to the waterfront. The little church of St Nicholas dates back to around the 11th and 12th century. A guide can be purchased inside for 10p.

2. Immediately opposite the Ship Inn go up the track to the Itchenor Sailing Club. The path follows the coast then heads inland and out into a lane. Turn left walking past some impressive looking properties until you reach the signed footpath on the right. At first it runs beside a bluebell wood then heads across the field to meet a track on the far side.

3. Turn left through the farm, down the drive, out through the entrance gate and turn immediately right, the path is signed. Go into the field and walk round keeping close to the hedge on the right. After diverting to the right round the end of the hedge the path continues ahead round the field, it is all well signed from here. At the junction of two paths cross the ditch then go over the small ditch into the caravan park and across to meet the drive following it through the park, out into the road and turn left.

4. At the road junction cross over and walk down towards Huntland & Guys Farm. Bear right into the field then cross into the adjoining field. Further ahead cross the ditch on the right and follow the path beside the hedge then bear right across the field to the hedge, up to the farm and turn right onto the drive. A short distance down turn left into the field. The path is liable to be wet and often becomes overgrown in the summer. Turn right onto the lane, then right again at the crossroads back to the inn.

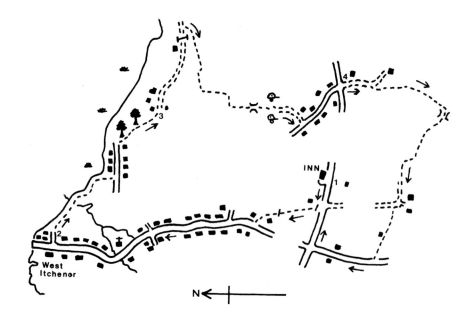

West
Itchenor

N